1/20

Stories on Rye

Published by Pomelo & Co.
P.O. Box 411272
Los Angeles, CA 90041

Library of Congress Cataloging-in-Publication Data is available.

Designed & illustrated by Gina Canter
Cover design by Gina Canter & Jaya Nicely

ISBN: 978-1-7338431-0-2

Manufactured in Canada

First Edition

1 3 5 7 9 10 8 6 4 2

Stories on Rye

Gina Canter & Alex Canter
Illustrated by Gina Canter

FOREWORD

Cities are often defined by places—the spots on a map that become the heart of our neighborhoods. These are destinations that fill in the landscape and feel like home. For Los Angeles, Canter's is one of those iconic landmarks.

For countless Angelenos, Canter's is more than a place to grab a pastrami on rye or a bowl of matzo ball soup—it's a second dining room. You look around the restaurant and see families in nearby booths, friends walking through the door, and familiar faces in the kitchen. Grabbing a quick bite may be the reason for someone's first visit to Canter's, but the sense that you are part of a family keeps folks coming back.

Los Angeles is a place where everybody is welcome. Canter's embodies this spirit, and perhaps that's because for close to 90 years Canter's has grown up alongside our city — from its early days in Boyle Heights to its long-standing home on Fairfax.

Stories on Rye brings to life more than 100 reflections that capture what it means to dine at Canter's. There are families torn apart by the Holocaust being reunited, and young Angelenos falling in love during the graveyard shift. All of the stories have one thing in common — and that's Canter's—because this is a deli that brings people together.

Growing up in Los Angeles, the center of culinary gravity often brought me to Canter's. Sometimes it was for a family meal, and at other times it was a late-night meet-up with friends. But no matter what was on the table, or who was around it, I always felt at home at Canter's.

This book is so much more than a loose collection of stories. It is a reminder that here in the City of Angels, we don't just mark history—we make history. And since 1931, Canter's has done just that by opening its doors to all Angelenos and connecting our hearts through our stomachs.

Eric Garcetti
Mayor of Los Angeles

In loving memory of Alan Canter and Gary Canter

INTRODUCTION

Los Angeles was a far different place when our great-grandfather, Ben Canter, opened Canter's Deli in 1931. Hollywood was just getting started and a cute little mouse named Mickey was becoming a star.

Ben opened Canter's Deli in Boyle Heights, the "Jewish Shtetl" of Los Angeles, and in 1948 he moved the deli to its present home on Fairfax Avenue, alongside 15 other Jewish delis and a growing Jewish community. To keep up with demand, our family added a second dining room in the 1950s.

What began as a small deli selling ethnic food to regular folks, is today an iconic Los Angeles landmark, a world-famous hangout for celebrities, musicians and politicians.

Looking Back

After the move to Fairfax Avenue, the new upstairs banquet room became home to many special events, such as birthday parties, weddings, and bar-mitzvahs. Celebrities and major politicians were frequently spotted there, among them JFK.

The Sixties in Los Angeles was the era of the Rat Pack, hippies, and a fast-growing music scene reflected in the explosive growth of the

Sunset Strip. To meet the late-night demands of the hippie crowd, our family added a cocktail bar, the Kibitz Room, next door to the restaurant, and decided to keep Canter's open 24/7. Since it was one of the few places open all night, the counterculture crowd descended on Canter's, including regulars like The Doors, Janis Joplin, James Brown and many others.

With its central location, and deep ties to the community, Canter's was naturally a second home to many politicians including city councilmen, mayors, and presidents alike. Knowing its historic importance, in 1973 Tom Bradley chose Canter's as the place to announce his candidacy to run as the city's first black mayor.

Throughout the Seventies and Eighties, Canter's was a go-to hangout for the hardworking industry crowd—the place to be seen for film producers, screenplay writers, comedians, and actors including Michael Mann, Nicolas Cage and Rodney Dangerfield. This has not changed, even as deli culture started to fade in the Nineties, and Jewish Delis nationwide began closing their doors. In fact, of the 15 Jewish Delis that were once located on Fairfax, Canter's is the only one that remains.

Stepping into Canter's is like stepping into a time machine. The old-school bakery counter, 1950s décor, and mod light fixtures create a retro ambiance that can't be replicated anywhere. For this reason, Canter's continues to be used as a film set for TV shows and movies set in all eras including *Mad Men, Curb Your Enthusiasm, Entourage, Transparent, The Disaster Artist*, and *Be Cool*, to name a few. We remember the location scout for *Mad Men* telling us that filming at Canter's was the easiest set design for their entire season—all they had to do was remove the ketchup bottles from the table to make it look like the Sixties.

It's a Family Affair

Over the past few decades, Canter's has won awards for Best Pastrami and other delicacies, but it's not just the food that keeps our heartbeat strong. We pride ourselves on continuing as a family-owned and operated business. We've always taken matters into our own hands, and that's been the secret to our longevity.

We have vivid memories of our grandpa, Papa Alan, waking early every morning to prepare the fruit cups. He always wanted to make sure that the fruit was perfectly ripe and served properly.

Today, our Aunt Jacqueline runs around in the early morning hours pouring coffee for our regulars, and our father, Marc, continues to work

15+ hour days, and has done so for as long as we can remember. He's on-call 24/7, which explains why he wasn't able to attend either of our college graduations! But we weren't disappointed because we knew he considers that to be the sacrifice needed to keep the doors open.

Canter's Today

Today, Canter's is regarded as an institution in Los Angeles because of its unique history. It is one of the oldest, and largest restaurants in the country. The restaurant on Fairfax occupies 30,000 square feet and employs 180 full-time people. Millions of people have passed through our deli doors since they opened in 1931.

Growing up as fourth-generation family members of Canter's Deli gave us a unique perspective on the business. Just as our father, grandfather, and great-grandfather did before us, we both started working in the restaurant at a very young age. We started waiting tables at age 11, and even then knew that we were being tasked with the responsibility to carry the restaurant forward for the next generation. As we've grown up we've taken on more responsibilities—from 15-hour shifts every Christmas, to updating the menu, to making it possible for customers to order Canter's online.

We're honored to be part of the Canter's story and we love to hear people's stories about the deli. Wherever we travel, people enjoy telling us their treasured Canter's tales. It usually starts with "That one time in 1976..." or "My grandparents used to take me there as a kid and now I take my grandchildren."

We've had the extraordinary privilege of interacting with thousands of Canter's employees, first-timers, regulars, celebrities, politicians, and everyone in between. As we listened to our family's history through other people's memories, we realized that the Canter's story was so much bigger than our own story. It is actually comprised of decades of memories, and countless people, from all walks of life.

This book is a collection of your stories since we first opened in 1931. We dedicate this book to everyone who has helped keep our doors open all these years.

We're honored to intertwine our Canter's Deli family history with yours.

—Gina Canter and Alex Canter, 4th generation

Ben Canter, Founder of Canter's Deli, 1963

SHOP
CANTER
DELICAT
2323
CANTER
Leader
BARBER SHOP
CANTER BROS
STEAKS CHOPS
DELICATESSEN

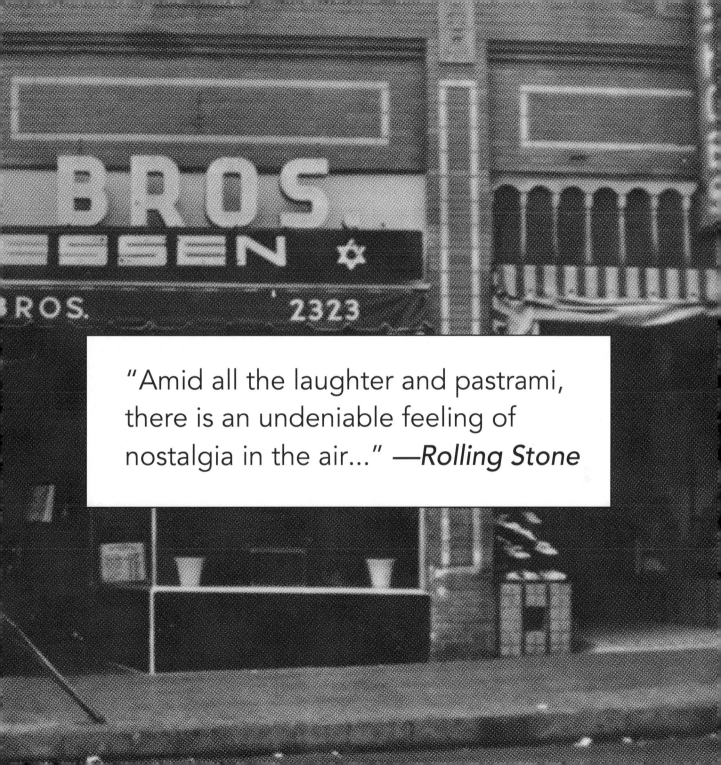

"Amid all the laughter and pastrami, there is an undeniable feeling of nostalgia in the air..." —*Rolling Stone*

"Coming to Canter's with my family has been my pleasure for many, many years. As a Holocaust survivor, I enjoy meeting other people who have gone through a similar experience. I am treated like royalty by the wonderful Canter's family who refer to me as "a best customer." The hostess and waiters treat me as though I am a celebrity. I am always greeted by my first name and treated to a plate of delicious pastries. I enjoy the food and appreciate all of the attention given to me considering my past. During the Holocaust, I worked in a coal mine. Back then, if you didn't dig enough coal, you did not get your ration of bread and soup. Now, here I am at Canter's being treated like royalty."

Charles, age 99

"I have been making sandwiches at Canter's for fifty-four years. I remember when Wilt Chamberlain would walk in with no shoes in the middle of the night and he would look behind the deli counter to see if I was in. He would only eat If I was making his sandwich. Jerry Lee Lewis would eat fat corned beef on a kaiser roll. He also would only eat if I was working. I once saw Muhammad Ali eating in station three. I went to the bathroom during my break and there he was in the bathroom with me. I had to help him, as he had Parkinson's at this time. I have seen it all.

I became very close to the Canter's family. Back in the day, I would fight about the way the pickles should be prepped with Ben Canter, the original owner. Years later, I would pick avocados with Alan Canter, Ben's son, at his house. In 1989, I watched Marc Canter walk down the aisle. And today, I'm still behind the deli, making the same sandwiches of 1964."

George

"Canter's is a lifestyle. The last twelve years I have come in sick, sad, hungry, full, drunk, mourning, all of it. I've shared pickles with Angelyne. I've taken dates here to see them under the bright tree ceiling. I've read numerous books in an anonymous corner while nomming on a pastrami reuben with no Russian dressing. I have slurped matzah ball soup at the front counter with my sick eyes swollen shut. And every damn time I get the service you can't get anywhere in LA or the planet. Straightforward, real humans, some with more pizazz and others that are like your grand-mother. And obviously the friken food keeps me fat and happy. You are my twenty-four-hour heaven and I love you."

Dylan, age 28

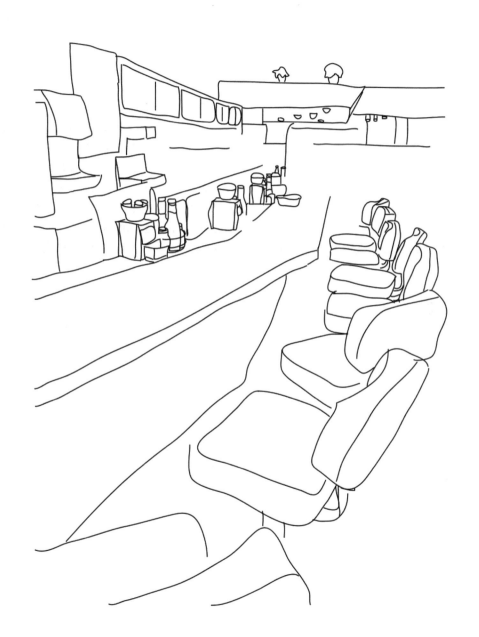

"My partner and I were Prince's first managers. We worked hard producing his demo tapes in Minneapolis. We came to LA in the spring of 1978 to promote Prince's work and sign him to a record deal. The first evening in LA, I insisted we come to Canter's for a great corned beef sandwich. Prince had never had one before. Our waitress brought out sandwiches and, as Prince was about to slather his sandwich in ketchup, I informed him he had to stop immediately and use mustard instead. I had to promise to replace the sandwich if he didn't like the mustard. Needless to say, he loved it."

Gary, age 73

"I came to Los Angeles for the same reason most do; to pursue my acting and film-making career. I moved in the late summer of 2014, and one day while looking for jobs in Hollywood, I stumbled into the famous Canter's Deli. I loved the food so much I started to come every day and quickly became a regular. As luck would have it, a position was open as a busboy. I took it and was hired on the spot. Although I found another job that took me away from Canter's, I would always find a reason to stop in. After a year of struggling in Hollywood, and the jobs being few and far between, I moved back to my home state of Oklahoma.

Canter's always gave me an open door to return. They knew I would be back. Fast forward two and a half years and boom I moved back to Hollywood. I started coming to my favorite deli and it was like I never left. They remembered my name and even my usual. It was home.

David, age 27

"I come to Canter's all the time, so it's hard to pick one story. But here are a few:

1. I fell asleep while eating a Rueben here after a night out with friends. When they woke me up, I remember feeling so happy Canter's was open all night. I could eat Rueben's here forever.

2. When I was a delivery driver, a person ordered soup from Canter's. I remember thinking whoever ordered must be a good person if they were getting soup from Canter's.

3. I ordered pancakes here every Sunday morning for like three months. I had to diet for my wedding which is why I stopped. I'm married now so I may go for the record.

Grace, age 27

"My boyfriend brought me to Canter's for the first time in the late 80s. Not being an 'adventurous' eater, I ordered a pastrami sandwich. He ordered the tongue sandwich. 'Yuck!' I thought to myself…The food came and we started in on our sandwiches. My boyfriend says, 'this cut of tongue is super-thin…' I looked down at my sandwich and realized I had been eating the tongue sandwich! From that day forward, we referred to that event as 'the time the waiter slipped me the tongue—and I liked it!'"

Sigrid, age 49

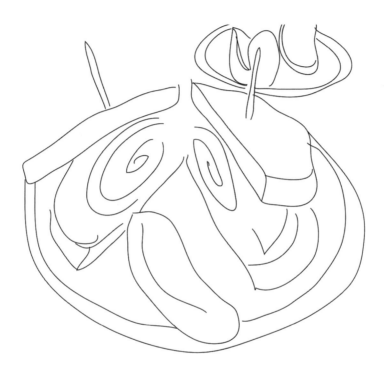

"Our family immigrated here from England in 1956, leaving most of our family behind. In 1963 we moved into the Fairfax district. Canter's Deli became a favorite place for my parents to eat.

One day, while dining at Canter's, my mother looked over to a booth not far from where they were sitting and thought she had seen a ghost. Sitting there, was a man the spitting image of her deceased father. Curiosity got the better of her, so she approached him and introduced herself. After much discussion, she discovered that the man she was talking to was a long-lost cousin from Poland who was imprisoned in a concentration camp during World War II. His name was Sam and was the son of her uncle (her father's brother) in Poland. Sam and his wife lived in the valley.

This chance meeting led to many milestone celebrations with them and their family. We celebrated Bar and Bat Mitzvahs, holidays, and my parents 50th wedding anniversary which was held at Canter's in, what used to be, an upstairs banquet hall.

Canter's has been a gathering place for our family for many years and hopefully for many more."

Vicienne, age 71

L.A. eateries enjoy a celebrity cli[entele]

l Granberry
Dallas Morning News

ELES — During a
hour at Canter's, a 52-
catessen on Fairfax
e heart of this city's
n neighborhood, two
eating lunch were
nsky and Jerry

s a great country or

hat it seemed to be
sual says everything
know about Canter's,
rs over the years
d Marilyn Monroe,
ylor and Muhammad
ing proof that those
e greatest in deli food
where to come.
e here, to this
odox community, for
nd pastrami sand-
half a pound high.
e for chicken mat-
which the menu
penicillin."
e for lox, eggs
rambled,
ish "that are
d," the wait-
d off with
t's most
rt —
rugu-

years,
ter's,
ling
ound it, has
uch as hair styles
en Canter's opened
uman was president.
e day, its Art-Deco
— the closest you'll
rmica Heaven — is
h regulars and
prefer the menu's
nigh-cholesterol
have graced Canter's
s.

at, it's a different
. It's a neon-
t-midnight corner
piked-haired, body-

fact that the marriage worked
about as well as *Stigmata* did at the
box office.)

Its adjoining nightclub, The
Kibbutz, is where Jacob Dylan,
Bob's son, started his very own
band, The Wallflowers. And that
kid you remember who's no longer
waiting tables? His new name is
Slash, and his employer is the
heavy-metal band, Guns 'N' Roses.

Some of the people Slash wait-
ed on may have a spot on its
patrons-of-the-past list, which
includes Sidney Poitier, Mel
Brooks, the late Wilt Chamberlain,
Charlene Tilton of *Dallas*, Brooke
Shields, Jacqueline Bisset, John
Travolta, Prince, Stevie Wonder,
Buddy Hackett, Olivia Newton-
John, Bill Cosby, David Brenner,
Rodney Dangerfield, Dick Van
Dyke, the late Elizabeth
Montgomery, and, of course,
Ms. Lewinsky and Mr.
Springer.

But serv-
ing

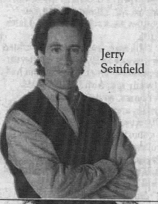

Jerry Springer

as a lunch counter for a *Who's
Who* of Hollywood is not the reason Canter's exists, argues Ms.
Canter, who traces its staying
power to its stiff-necked originali-
ty.

"We pickle our own pickles,"
she says, as if disclosing a state
secret. "You can always tell a fake
Jewish deli from a real one by asking about the turkey. If it's real,
fresh-roasted turkey like ours,
then it's a real Jewish deli. But if
it's pressed, it's a fake deli. Trust
me, I know."

■

Not too far from Canter's in dis-
tance but a world apart in every

Jerry
Seinfield

other way is The Ivy, on North
Robertson. Don't be surprised to
walk in and see Jerry Seinfeld sitting at the table next to yours.

At the same time, don't be
shocked if they ask you to leave
for taking his picture or having
him sign your napkin. Not that
anyone does. It just ain't kosher at
The Ivy. Try it and they'll be every
bit as friendly as the Soup Nazi.

At one of L.A.'s most popular
restaurants — it routinely makes
the city's top 10 of "power lunch"
hot spots — they don't just respect,
they *police* your privacy, even
more so if you're a studio mogul or
the mega-star of one of TV history's most popular laughathons.

Oh, and one more thing: The
food is good. On most days, really,
really good.

Richard Irving, co-owner and
executive chef, was one of the first
outside the city's African-
American community to serve
Cajun-style dishes and Louisiana
seafood on a daily basis.

But The Ivy is hardly limited to
that.

The 20-year-old restaurant
(which has a much beachier sister
location in Santa Monica) tries to
keep it simple, Mr. Irving says,

Va[let]
Park[ing]
$3.50

The Ivy mair

relying heavil
and fish and h
if he *had* to pl
prefers Louisi
corn chowder
prepared with

Those who
crave its barbe
(accompanied
shrimp), whic
mesquite-grill
zucchini and l

"It's what 6
guests order a[t]

Canter, left, and Harold Price: son and son-in-law, respectively, of the founder of Canter's.

THE SOUL OF FAIRFAX AVENUE

anter's moved
and has been ke...

...LAH BERNSTEIN
...TO THE TIMES

...ty-odd years ago, when
...wish neighborhood an...
...as on Brooklyn Aven...
...step in at the deli fo...
...pastrami sandwich
...n egg cream. He
...settle into one of
...oths with his Uncle
...sometimes he would...
...uch to go for his fa...
...who ran Zellman's
...wear across the

...ay, of course, Can-
...s long since moved
...that Avenue and Zell-
...s the last of the
...al Jewish stores in
...Heights. But that
...stop Dean Zellman
...wishful thinking. "I
...go for a corned beef
...ch right now on a
...roll"

...ly, who couldn't
...n Canter's moved to
...airfax area in 1948,
...lanting those salty
...le deli smells, it was
...g a demographic
...nat had begun a few
...earlier. Fairfax
...ward between Mel-
...venue and Beverly
...ard was becoming
...w Jewish hot spot.
...ry of Canter's can
...plain how Los An-
...ewish community adopted Fairfax as home.
...Canter, son of one of the original Canter's
...started as a pickle packer and delivery boy
...Fairfax store. Now 62, he remembers when
...usiness lined the street and how a neigh-
...od developed, thanks to heavy pedestrian

Above, the Boyle Heights Canter's, 1936.
Below, the Fairfax Canter's today.

"It was an up-and-com-
ing Jewish neighborhood,
with plenty of room for expansion," says 78-year-old
Harold Price, Canter's
brother-in-law, who helped
establish the eatery's Fairfax location.

At the time, the neigh-
borhood boasted Fairfax
High School and the Farm-
ers Market, the Esquire theater and Billy Gray's Band
Box, a flashy comedy club.
Also Cohen's deli, a bakery
or two and the Fairfax theater on Beverly Boulevard,
which attracted huge
crowds.

In the late 1930s and
'40s, the Fairfax Jewish
community kept growing as families arrived from
Boyle Heights and City Terrace, Los Angeles' Jewish centers since the early part of the century.

In 1931, before this population shift, Ben, Joe
and Ruby Canter opened Canter Bros. Delicatessen on Brooklyn Avenue (now East Cesar E.
Chavez Avenue), offering pickled herring and

always sit in the same back booth
and usually order a platter of lox,
whitefish and smoked cod with
cream cheese, bagels, lettuce,
tomatoes and onions.

For the older generation of folks
who had established businesses
downtown, the streetcar system
made commuting between the east
and west ends of town easy. Lynn
C. Kronzek, author of "Fairfax: A
Home, a Community, a Way of
Life," writes that it became increas-
ingly possible to seek "upward, yet
affordable, mobility."

So in 1948, Ben Canter and his
best friend, Hymie Fisch, bought
property on Fairfax Avenue: two
connecting storefronts that became
the new Canter's location. Their
children ran the business—this
time designed as a combination
restaurant, deli and bakery—at 439
N. Fairfax, next door to where
Schwartz Bakery stands today.

The original Canter's hung on in
Boyle Heights until the early 1970s,
but over the years, many of its
Brooklyn Avenue neighbors, including Leader Barber Shop,
moved to Fairfax too.

In 1953, Canter's moved into the
Esquire theater building at 419 N.
Fairfax and became a 24-hour
restaurant, one of the first in the
city. In 1959, it expanded north,
buying out Cohen's deli next door.
And in 1961, the Kibitz Room
opened as a cocktail lounge that
has attracted all sorts of scene
makers through the years, from Jim
Morrison to Courtney Love.

On a morning visit to Canter's,
it's easy to see why customers keep
returning and employees never
seem to leave. It is a home away
from home. The food may have
changed a bit, the street may ap-
pear unkempt, more diners may
show up with neon-colored hair...

"Some regular customers have the same thing every morning. One couple from Bel Air said, 'It's like home. When we're away, we come here right off the plane.'"

—*Beverly Hills Courier*

"Attending Fairfax High School, all the cool kids spent first period at Canter's. It was the 80s so it was mainly to use the upstairs bathrooms to put on shocking makeup, re-pierce those nose/upper ear piercings, put on racy garb and get ready without giving your parents a heart-attack! Me and my friends were smart because we knew the Kibitz Room had its own bathroom and we didn't have to wait to get in front of the mirror. So, every morning we'd just pop in, grab a bagel and a coffee from the deli counter, and walk it over to the piano bar of the Kibitz Room. We would stare straight across both dining rooms to see the mayhem of kids running around there. I mean, there was a line of kids all the way up and down those stairs to the bathrooms. I remember it as if it was a class I took!

Fast forward to the late 80s, as clockwork every night, I was in that dreaded line to be seated in the dining room to smoke countless cigarettes and dip fat fries in gravy. I was always making the rounds to different tables since I knew half of LA and was meeting all the newbies that were flocking to Hollywood at the time. So, this one night, a friend of mine (Ethan) saw me in line and said I have to meet his friend that's looking for a keyboardist. As we walked out of the main dining room and passed the second dining room, we entered the Kibitz Room! And there in the only booth with people in it is Jakob Dylan and the rest of the early Wallflowers lineup. My opening line was "What the hell are you guys doing in HERE? This is where my dad comes to drink!"

Rami Jaffee, Keyboardist of Foo Fighters

"More than fifty years ago, our parents started taking us to Canter's every week. They had been going many years before we came along. Dad would stop by Canter's weekly to bring home goodies from the bakery. Over the years it became a place to take our children and now grandchildren. That's four generations of one family who loves Canter's. It seemed only fitting that after leaving the mortuary to finalize mom's funeral arrangements in 2015, we all stopped at Canter's for lunch. It was one little way to quickly recapture a lifetime of memories."

Michael

"No matter where we've lived, whenever we visit Los Angeles, we always make time to eat at Canter's. We came to Canter's over forty years ago for our first pastrami sandwich. We couldn't help but notice all the old people eating there.

Today, while eating a pastrami sandwich, we realized we are now the old people."

Michael and Debra

"I have a story from 1971 about getting kicked out of Fairfax Theater for being rambunctious. My parents had to pick me up and we went to Canter's afterwards; I was in a lot of trouble. We picked up deli food in silence before going home. We went to Canter's a lot anyway."

Slash, Guns N' Roses

"Many late nights were spent after the local punk rock shows at Canter's. They were unusually punk friendly. At that time punk rock was not that well known. We were looked at as scary dressed-up freaks. The staff didn't know what to make of us, but they were always warm and friendly. I would choose between the kasha knish or corned beef on Rye, finish it up around 3:00am and then go straight to bed."

Belinda Carlisle, Singer of the Go Go's

"I have been coming to Canter's since I was a child. In June of 2015, I was diagnosed with breast cancer and had to undergo surgery, chemotherapy and radiation. During my hospital stay, my husband would order my meals from Canter's to raise my spirits up. Canter's matzah ball soup is a healer. During my chemo treatments, my husband brought me directly here right after my infusions. He knew the food here would make me feel better and it was the only food I could stomach. I credit Canter's Deli for keeping me well fed and healthy through my cancer treatments."

Keani, age 41

"I am fourty-seven.

I've been going to Canter's for forty-five of those years.

As a young child Canter's always meant Black & Whites on a Saturday night.

As a teen, Canter's meant the best fries in town on a Saturday night.

As a parent, Canter's still feels like home any night of the week!

Any time we have out-of-towners who enjoy great food and service by real professionals we bring them to Canter's!

Thank you to the Canter's family for being our family!"

Malinda

"In a crazy way I owe my life to this deli. In March of 1980, my mother, Candy, was a waitress at Canter's. She was working the graveyard shift. My father and his friends came in for a late-night bite. And the rest is history. Seven months later they eloped. Thirteen years later, I came along. I've even eaten in the booth where it all began and it's WILD. So, thanks Canter's."

Simone

Canter's Deli Still Hip After Nearly 90 Years

by Heather Blount/*staff writer*

Which Jewish deli has been the set of "My Dinner with Jimi," "Curb Your Enthusiasm," "Enemy of the State" and "Entourage"?

The same one that attracts local residents from retirement homes, tourists from all over the world and Michael Mann, who spent several hours a day writing scripts in the deli, according to Jacqueline Canter, a manager at Canter's Deli in Los Angeles.

Canter says the deli has been the hot spot for celebrities since her grandfather, Ben Canter, opened the first location in Jersey City in 1924.

"Years ago, it used to be people like Marilyn Monroe and Arthur Miller who would come in. Now it's a little 'hipper' crowd," she says.

On the list of its patrons, past and present, are Scarlett Johansson, former New York Mayor Rudy Giuliani, Penelope Cruz, Dustin Hoffman, Gregory Peck, Mick Jagger, Al Pacino and Michael Jackson.

The deli's Kibitz Room, which was added in 1962, functions as a bar. That's where Nicolas Cage met Patricia Arquette, Jacob Dylan and The Wallflowers started their music career and artists from Ricky Lee Jones to The Red Hot Chili Peppers have performed.

Guns 'n Roses' famous (former) guitarist Slash used to work at Canter's, looking through the checks to make sure everyone was charged correctly.

Canter's brother grew up with Slash and "basically gave him a job," she says.

Slash also has played in the Kibitz Room with Guns 'n Roses, and still frequents Canter's as a customer.

Canter's Deli is a 24-hour restaurant and bakery in California.

While others fade, Canter's remains

"Kids who used to come when they were kids, they've now grown up and they bring their kids in because it's been here so many years. So the people that I remember when they were kids now have their own kids. Kinda sweet, actually," Canter says.

The family-run deli and bakery settled in Los Angeles in the Fairfax district in 1953, where it remains today. During that time, countless delis have gone

eration, she says. "And everybody in the family works here, so we're here every day to make sure that everything is run properly."

The 24-hour deli has 150 employees, and most of them have worked at Canter's for decades, she says. When she does need help, Canter looks for a "real waitress, not an actress."

By avoiding applicants who are "just killing time to get into the movies," the waitstaff develops a following of regular customers.

"We have the same employees forever," she says. "Most of them have been here 20 years, 30 years, 40 or 50."

In addition to the celebrity clientele, the deli draws from the Jewish neighborhood where it is located. There are retirement homes

Menu changes to suit the times

"After 80-something years in business, we decided it's time to change the menu because it's a healthier group of people that come here now than it used to be," Canter says.

> "Kids who used to come when they were kids, they've grown up and they bring their kids in because it's been here so many years. So the people that I remember when they were kids now have their own kids. Kinda' sweet, actually."
>
> — Jacqueline Canter

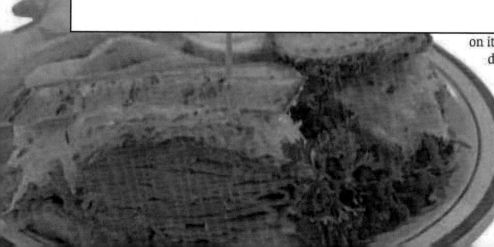

on its whereabouts so they can get the deli delights without traveling to Fairfax.

The Fairfax location has seen a few additions, including the Kibitz Room in 1962 and an adjacent parking lot in 1965, making the 14,000-s.f. delicatessen one of the largest in the country. In 2003, Canter's opened in the Treasure Island Hotel in Las Vegas and, in 2008, a location opened in Dodger Stadium; both locations have since closed, leaving

"In 1952, my grandfather brought me to Canter's on Brooklyn Avenue for the first time. Years later I got married and started bringing my wife and children. That started in 1969, and has not stopped to this date. As each of our children married, they continued coming here along with almost all of our nineteen grandchildren. That makes four generations so far. We have come to Canter's every Christmas for dinner for the past twenty-five years. What more can I say but thanks to Canter's for being here for so long. Bella has always been one of our favorite people, watching all of our kids grow up. She always comes to our booth to say hello when we are here."

Joel, age 71

"Way back in 1988 my friend Julie and I were at Canter's late night as usual after work. We were enjoying our matzah ball soup and potato knish with gravy, and guess who is sitting at a table a few feet from us? A very young and handsome Nicholas Cage and pretty little Patricia Arquette. They were enjoying their meal, or at least trying to. People kept going up to them and asking for autographs. Nicholas would very gently put his fork down, smile, and sign napkins. Then he would try to take a bite and again a fan would approach him. He was so gracious to his fans. I have had several celebrity encounters over the years, but that one seems to be the most memorable. My family celebrates most holidays and birthdays there and have for over thirty years. We love Canter's! Can't leave without a Black & White cookie. Pastrami is THE BEST! Canter's is a very big part of our family traditions."

Joanna

"We 'Fairfax High' students would meet here most mornings for breakfast. You had a waitress we called 'Mama'. We, the ten of us, would order the usual stuff: pancakes, eggs, omelettes and so on. Mama would take the order and come back with what she thought we should have before going to school… oatmeal for all ten of us. Once in a while she would let us have what we really ordered."

Robert, age 56

"I moved (drove) here from Nashville, Tennessee with my parents and my one-year old daughter to start a new life. Canter's was the first restaurant in California that we stopped at. My family has been coming here ever since. In fact, I brought my son here for his high school graduation. Canter's is always a favorite with us. And we are back today 66 years later. Our whole family of four generations have been coming to Canter's—my two children, four grandchildren and the newest great-grandchild will be looking forward to the first visit."

Peggy, age 86

"I came here from Germany after surviving the Holocaust. I was twelve years old. I was so impressed that so many Jewish people could be so happy in one place. The last time I saw so many Jewish people together was in the camps. I love the food here, the atmosphere, the friendly faces, and the staff. I still come here to this day with my children and grandchildren. I share many fond memories of Canter's with my wife of sixty-one years. Never forget."

Jack, age 82

"The first time I heard of Canter's was from my grandmother. She told me she once saw Mel Brooks get up onto a table to sing and dance. I thought that was so cool. I was six years old and I wanted to go to Canter's so something cool like that would happen to me. Little did I know that I would end up eating more often at Canter's than any other restaurant in the world."

Colin, age 50

"I used to come to Canter's with my grandparents when I was four years old. It was always so crowded, it took a while to get a table. While we waited I used to walk along the ledge of the bakery and look at all the cookies. Then my grandma would buy me a box. The box was pink and still is. And I still come to Canter's to get those delicious cookies fifty years later. Good 'ole grandad used to let me dip my bagel and cream cheese in his coffee."

Alana, age 54

"We have been coming to Canter's for over two decades and it has been a tradition to take a picture under the front sign after we eat. We have amassed a collection of hundreds of photos with friends, family, and out-of-town visitors. The pictures chronicle our lives over the years and almost always include others walking by—other Canter's customers, Fairfax hipsters, men and women who are homeless, and Canter's waiters and waitresses taking breaks (including Fran, our favorite waitress). These pictures have been sent around the world and collected in books. As I write this we are getting ready to take yet another picture under the greatest sign in the world at LA's greatest restaurant."

Phillip, age 50

Canter's Avocado Mushroom Cheese Omelet

2 teaspoons butter

3 mushrooms, sliced

3 eggs, beaten

1 tablespoon water

Salt, pepper to taste

1/4 avocado, diced

2 ounces Swiss cheese, shredded

In 8-inch skillet over medium heat, melt butter, add mushrooms, saute until tender. Add eggs, beaten with water, salt and pepper. Over low heat, as mixture sets, with fork, draw this portion toward center so uncooked portions flow to bottom. Shake skillet to keep omelet sliding freely. When eggs are set but surface is still moist, sprinkle with avocado and cheese. With spatula, loosen edges of omelet. Carefully roll up omelet. Invert onto plate.

Makes 1 to 2 servings

nter's
ESTAURANT
CATESSEN BAKERY
ATESSEN
CANTER'S FAIRFAX DELICATESSEN & BAKERY
439

"My name is Kati Koster, and my Canter's memory is from July 24th, 2014. I'm the girl in the bright pink dress, sitting next to President Barack Obama. I wrote him a letter and I was chosen to speak with him.

It's amazing being incredibly starstruck for the first five minutes and barely being able to speak a coherent sentence; but President Obama has this magical way of making you feel comfortable, and like you are just speaking to a friend. He really listens, and he actually cares. Most amazing day of my life.

Also, the Black & White cookies are delicious!"

Kati

"My ex always told our friends that I bought my house down the street so I could be closer to Canter's. I have eaten at this cherished site for twenty-eight years. I could never sell my house because where would I eat?

My father would come to visit from Cleveland a couple of times a year and stay for a week. He would only eat at Canter's. My family comes to visit about once a year from Chicago. They will only eat at Canter's. We are waiting for the stock to become a public offering."

Maureen

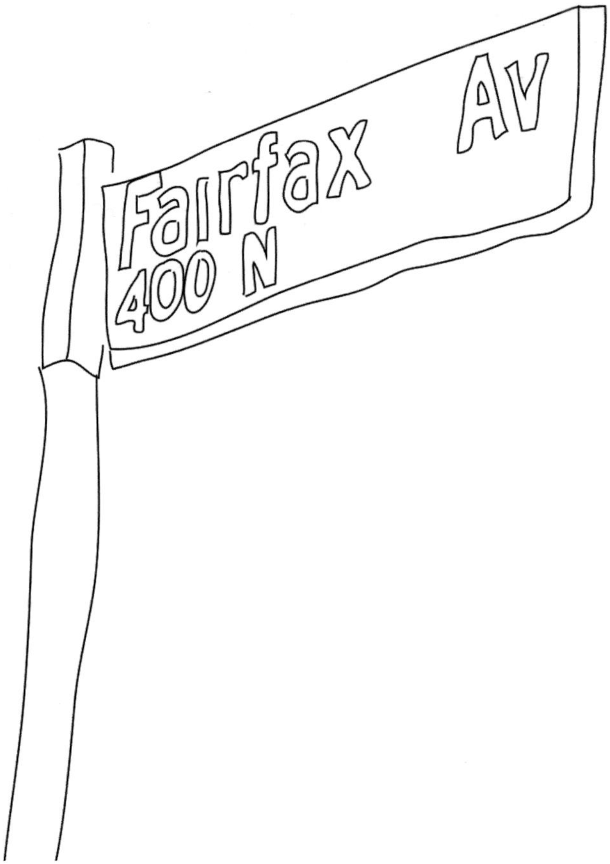
Fairfax Av
400 N

"When I was a doorman in Greenwich Village in 1966, I met a guy named 'Gypsy' who was the doorman at The Sea Witch on Sunset. I told him I was headed to L.A. and he told me that if I get there before 2:00am to go to Huff's and after 2:00am to go to Canter's. I got to Canter's around that time and had my first meal in Los Angeles. Not long after, I met the woman who would become my son's mother while standing in line for a table."

Jay

"When I started here in 1964, there was no Honda Center or Staples Center. I was a waitress for 20 years before I became the night shift manager. Selma Canter called me up and asked me to be the manager and I have been for the last 35 years. After about five months of working here, the whole place filled up with hippies. There used to only be four waitresses at night in that room, but once the hippies found Canter's, we needed ten waitresses. They would line out the door and lean on the windows. At least twice a night I would watch someone get up on the table and then get thrown out. I think they were on LSD. I started at 6pm and ended at 2am. But once the hippies came around I stayed till 4am. I couldn't leave when there was a line out the door. The only one I had a problem with was Rodney Dangerfield. After 2am he would pick a menu up and hide a beer in between the folds. I would say, 'What do you have there?' and he would say, "Nothing!' This was a routine. I would say 'Rodney, it's after 2am.' and I would take his beer away.

A more recent memory that I remember was when Bono came in. I didn't recognize him at the time. I just knew there was a concert that had just let out and it was around 2am. I remember going up to a waitress saying, 'Hey this party looks good do you want to take them?' This waitress responded, 'No I'm leaving in 10 minutes.' So I looked around and everyone seemed busy. I went over to them and said, 'I will find someone to wait on you but in the meantime can I get you started with anything?' This gentleman had an accent I wasn't familiar with and asked for what I thought he said were 'starches.' I guess he really said 'starters.' But I didn't figure that out until later. He told me to bring him anything I chose. Even though he didn't look Jewish, I brought him a Matzah Ball soup. He ate it up and said, 'I'm ready for my main, bring me whatever you think I will like.' I brought him a Reuben. Their check ended up being around $70 dollars. They left me a $150 tip. I thought he might have been famous, but I didn't figure it out until the next night. He gave me a shout out at his LA show the following night. In front of his entire crowd he said 'This waitress named Bella at Canter's Deli was the sweetest and brought me the best food.' That's when I realized I had just waited on U2.

Canter's has been my life for almost all my life. I am retiring March 28, 2019. I just recently attended Alan Canter's funeral. It's really something—I am retiring after 55 years within the same few weeks of Alan's passing. It feels like full circle. I remember when Alan and Elizabeth Canter were pregnant with their son Marc. Look, there's Marc behind the deli now…"

Bella, age 85

"I moved to LA in 1993 when I was twenty-three years old. After a few weeks couch surfing, I moved into an apartment on Spaulding. The first place I ate after moving in was Canter's.

As I walked in, I was amazed. I'm an Army brat and have lived in so many places—Germany, Florida, Virginia, Nashville, Philidelphia, but never in my life had I lived among fellow Jews. And never, ever had I lived in a place where Matzah Brie was on the menu of a restaurant around the corner from my home.

Between late night Matzah Brie and Matzah Ball Soup when I was sick, Canter's became a favorite.

Today is my first day back since 1998. This time I'm with my husband and my son. I took a single bite of a pickle and started crying. 'It's nostalgia!' my son said. He wasn't wrong."

Lisa-Anne, age 48

"I was born half Jewish on my dad's side, meaning I'm not a 'real Jew'. Regardless of how much I wanted to be accepted by the community, I never felt welcome by certain family members. So, when people would joke and say, 'You're not a real Jew because you never had a Jewish mom', it hurt. But ever since I was little, my dad would remedy my worries by taking me to Canter's at least once a month. He had been coming here since he was eleven years old, back in the early 50s.

I would always hear people talking about how nothing can ever beat grandma's cooking. I never met my grandmother on my Jewish side as she passed away before I was born. I always thought of Canter's as being my Jewish Grandma.

I live in New York now, and I constantly argue that Canter's is better than any other deli in town. I stand by that."

Sarah, age 27

"I have lived in the Fairfax neighborhood my whole life and have grown up going to Canter's with friends. Today, it's June 7th 2018, and it's the last day of our junior year. Last year, we (Leo, Alfie and I) ditched our last day of school and came here for breakfast. Here we are again this year! We are already planning to be back next year for our annual School's Out breakfast! Thanks for feeding us our first meals of summer for the past two years."

Lila, age 16

"We had come in way after 2:00am and sat at the soda fountain counter. The waitress was a tall blonde, older. I ordered a banana split. With hand on hip she said 'I'm not making a banana split at this hour.' I LOVE this memory."

Louis, age 62

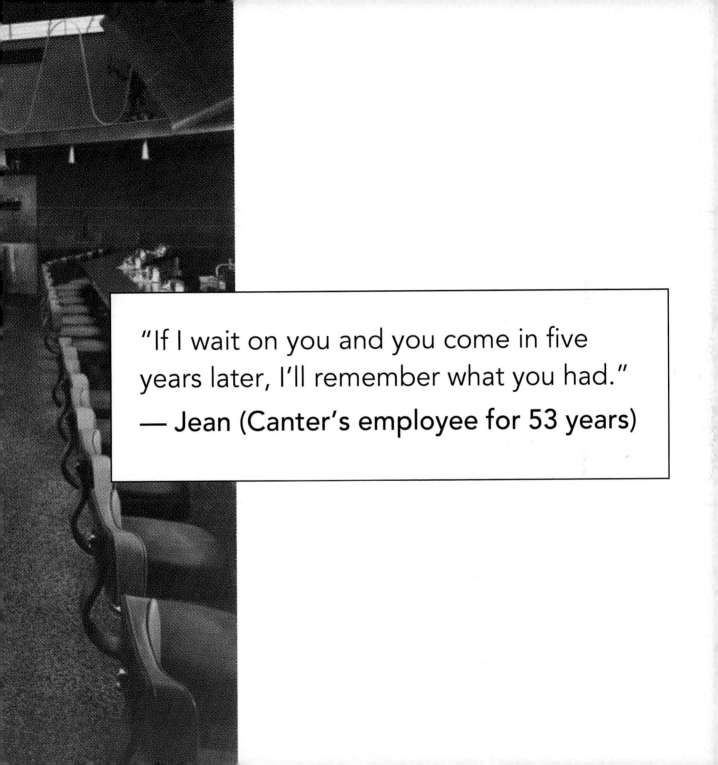

"If I wait on you and you come in five years later, I'll remember what you had."

— Jean (Canter's employee for 53 years)

"When I was a teenager in the seventies Bella would chase us out one door. We would come in the other door late at night and she would tell us to go home but we would sneak back in, find a seat, and act like we were always there. She would find us in the bar then kick us out for the night. This went on for quite some time. Bella was one of the youngest at the time and to this day when she sees me asks if my sister and I are getting along. It's funny all the waitresses were cranky and loud but were so awesome."

Meryl (Koko)

"The year was 1994 and I was in my freshman year at USC. My brother, my aunt, my parents and my grandparents were up from the OC, as they were most Sundays to visit me. Our ritual was set. We ate in the first booth in the second room, as it was always less crowded and could accommodate the seven of us. On this day, we ordered our usual half sandwich and soup specials and my grandpa's big New Yorker. It was a pretty normal day. While the rest of us headed to the bakery, my grandpa sat on the front bench in the other room. All of a sudden everything began to shake. We were in the middle of an earthquake. My grandpa who could barely walk (he had two canes) comes running, like really running. And that went down in family lore, that if grandpa really needed to move, he really could."

Elizabeth, age 43

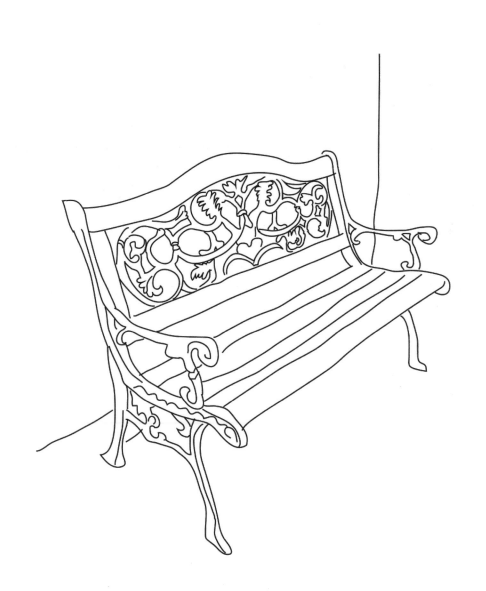

"I have been coming here since I was five years old. I am originally from Chicago. My father's sister moved here from Brooklyn. We would come here just off the plane. My dad would purchase every baked good in the place to lavish my sister. I come back to visit twice a year. This is my first stop. Matzo brei and chocolate chip rugelach. Now all five of my kids proudly wear their Canter's T-shirts. Plus, I have to bring home five pounds of rugelach. This place reminds me of my father, Irving Zelig Houmen. This was his favorite place.

Six years ago, I was here with my youngest son, Nathaniel. We had the nicest waiter, Andy. My son has Down Syndrome. Andy was enamored with Nate's intelligence and kindness. Nate wrote Andy a little note: 'Hi Andy, I love you, Nate'. Nate was eight years old. A few years later I was here alone. Andy was my server again and he remembered me. Andy reached for his wallet and pulled out the note from my son. I will never forget that. I cried from pride and pure happiness. That is what Canter's means to me.

P.S This is also the only place that knows what a water bagel is. Mazel."

Holly, age 53

"I met my wife Tana in 1987 in my home state, Texas. Standing in line at Jason's Deli, she said, 'This isn't really a deli. If you want real deli food you have to go to Canter's in LA.' Being from a state that never lets the truth get in the way of a good story, I thought 'sure!' In 1988 she brought me to Canter's. I hate to admit it but she was right. I had never really had real deli. Every time we are in LA, we come to Canter's. Definitely one of my happy places."

Larry, age 58

"I remember coming to Canter's in 1992 after opening for Janes Addiction at the Palace. We were young and rock was king back then. Canter's was the go to restaurant for all musicians to hit after their local gigs. I went up into the girl's bathroom to fix my makeup. To my surprise, members of Guns N' Roses and Janes Addiction were also in the girl's bathroom putting their makeup on too. Good times."

Inger, age 48

"I graduated from Fairfax High in 1963. During my senior year, my friends and I walked home every day after school because my girlfriend lived in the apartment building right behind Canter's (it's still there). We would always stop at Canter's along the way. At other schools, it might have been an after-school burger and coke, but for us it was a knish and a coke. Served by the same waitress everyday who always called us 'dearie.' Canter's was home fifty-five years ago and still is today."

Andy, age 72

"When I was six-years-old, my parents and I moved from Brooklyn New York to Los Angeles. My parents took me to Canter's. I stood in front of the restaurant and asked my parents if Eddie Cantor, the comedian, owned this restaurant. I turned around to get their answer, and a man who was walking by said, 'No, but I wish I did.' It was Eddie Cantor walking with his wife. It was a memory I will never forget. Every time I go to Canter's I think of that moment in 1952 when I met Eddie Cantor in front of the restaurant."

Joan

"I had just moved to Los Angeles from Boston. I was a recent college grad who wanted to work in the entertainment industry, but also needed to be as far away from home as possible, to finally figure out who I was and live my life authentically. That evening, still in the dial-up days of the Internet, I logged online and pulled up a chatroom for gay men...even though I was petrified. Oprah had been warning her viewers not to talk with people online, as chat rooms could potentially be filled with crazy serial killers! Despite this, I felt desperate to make (gulp) gay friends, having lived in the closet for so many years. A 'chat invite' suddenly popped up, asking if I'd like to have a 'private' conversation with some-one named James. I accepted, and we began chatting. James had moved to LA from Australia only six months prior, also eager to be far enough away from home where he could live freely, as an out gay man. We eventually transitioned the conversation from computer-to-telephone, and the dialog continued to flow easily for hours, filled with kindness, humor, and ease. I had never felt so myself, and so understood, so I decided to take a second major risk: I asked James, who actually went by Jimmy, if he'd like to meet in person...that same evening. It was already pretty late, but I felt an emotional pull that I couldn't explain or resist. I had struggled being myself for so many years, feeling so isolated in the process, that I figured I had nothing to lose. Living in Park LaBrea, Jimmy suggested Canter's Deli as a place for us to meet. Having heard of Canter's but never having been there before, I agreed, as it sounded like a place that serial killers were hopefully unlikely to frequent. I headed over, praying for the best. I pulled my car into Canter's parking lot and walked towards the front door, heart-in-throat. I saw a nice-looking guy waiting outside the front door.

'Hi, are you Jimmy?'
'I am, you must be Tom?'

The kind smiles we shared immediately put us at ease. Both in our early twenties, we were pretty broke and ordered modestly... a vanilla milkshake for Jimmy, guac and chips for me. At one point Jimmy commented on how big my smile was. I know the reason for that: sitting in that incredibly compact booth in Canter's Deli, I had never felt happier or freer in my entire life. On the ten-year anniversary of the night we met at Canter's, we legally got married in a strip mall in Van Nuys, shortly after CA began recognizing same-sex marriage. Afterwards, we headed to Canter's for a celebration meal, exactly ten years after that first serendipitous night we met. Fully ready to become dads, we decided to take the adoption route and welcomed the birth of our son Lukas. Shortly after we our welcomed our daughter Maya into our lives. Just a couple weeks shy of our twentieth anniversary, we flew out to LA and headed back to that same magical booth in Canter's Deli, to celebrate the first two decades of our love story. I couldn't help but keep back the tears that were filled with joy and pride...Canter's is where our amazing journey began."

Tom & Jimmy

Los Angeles

APRIL 9, 2008

RESTAURANT JOURNAL

Catcher and the deli rye

VIN Scully's voice reverberated through Dodger Stadium at a recent rainy-night game against the visiting Giants, while hungry fans stocked up on hot dogs and beer, nachos and cotton candy — and matzo ball soup, courtesy of Canter's Deli's newly opened concession stand.

In time to mark the team's 50th-anniversary celebrations, the Dodgers unveiled a serious upgrade to the field level when the season opened last week. In addition to Canter's Deli, which is on the third-base side, new concessions include Mrs. Beasley's, Camacho's Cantina and Ruby's Diner.

It's only the second expansion in Canter's history. The family-run business opened in 1924 in New Jersey and moved to Los Angeles in 1931. In 2003, Canter's opened an outpost in Las Vegas, at the Treasure Island Hotel.

A Canter's at Chavez Ravine is a perfect fit. The deli, which moved to Fairfax Avenue in 1953, is as much of an L.A. institution as Tommy Lasorda.

"Hey, is that *albondigas*?" one guy in full Dodger gear shouted in amazement, staring at his neighbor's squat paper cup of chicken broth, in which one enormous matzo ball floated, almost exactly the size of an errant fly ball.

David Breton of Seattle, a Mariners fan in town with his two young sons, was impressed — and it's not easy to impress a Safeco Field patron. (That stadium serves sushi.) "The best Jewish food I've ever had at a ballpark," said Breton, munching on a pastrami sandwich.

AMY SCATTERGOOD *Los Angeles Times*

SHORT STOP: *Deli food from Canter's is now at Dodger Stadium. The stand is on the third-base side.*

"But the soup needs a little salt."

The soup did need salt. And the sandwiches — pastrami, corned beef, a hybrid called a "Canter's Fairfax" (a mixture of the two meats on the same caraway-studded rye), and a turkey French dip — were in need of sauerkraut and mustard, neither of which the concession stand sells. (You can get mus-

lume 16, Number 2 • 14-20 Adar, 5761 • March 9-15, 2001 • www.jewishjournal.cc

FOODAISM

Celebrating the Venerable Delis of Los Angeles

Cant

THERE
delis, and
Steppin
Los Angel
seven-pa
wall. Four

> "Couples on dates also come here, as do 'parties of one': old men with books, young men with scripts, and young women—some with stylishly tilted hats."
>
> — *Los Angeles Times*

d War II Jewish
The Fairfax
ater, has since
ng room, a
n cocktail loun
/lan's band The

High Holy Day:
retirement-ho
these huddled
employees,
rs at Canter's,
which offers medical and dental benefits.

Alan Canter, son of a founding brother, still arrives
5 a.m. every morning to pick out fruit for the breakfast
plate, and nine third-generation cousins share manage
duties. Together, they serve up more than 6,000 gallon
chicken soup each month, along with 6.5 tons of corne
beef, pickled on the premises. Canter's full-service bak
produces the goods twice daily, donating the excess to
the local homeless.

When Jacqueline Canter started the Fairfax Busines
Association, which has fixed up the area's streets and
sidewalks, she did it to "bring the street back to the wa
remember it as a girl."

She adds, "This is something that's going to be here

"In 1970, I was seventeen years old and a student at Fairfax High school. Several friends and I lived near La Jolla Ave and Santa Monica Blvd. and walked to school each day (around 10 blocks). We hated school, and on many mornings, we would meet at Canter's for sodas and french fries. We were not the most respectful kids, although compared to kids in that category now...we were angels! At that time, it was legal to smoke in the restaurant and while we were not regular smokers, we felt safe in Canter's with all the kindly grandmothers watching over us! I imagine that we must have been a sight to the service staff, sixteen-year-old's and seventeen-year-old's trying to look cool while choking on cigarette smoke! Money was always an issue for us, however we never left without paying. We did not understand the concept of tips, so I guess the service staff suffered the most! I must confess, many years later that we took true delight in putting salt in the sugar shaker and sugar in the salt shaker. I also must confess that we never waited around to see what happened—we were too frightened of being caught! I do hope we did not hurt anyone!

We loved to sit in Canter's and people watch, many times, late at night (2:00am or 3:00 am). We would sit in a booth and watch the 'freak show'. At that time, Fairfax Ave. was being invaded by head shops ('hippy' psychedelic shops selling black lights, incense, rock and roll posters of Jimmy Hendrix and so many others). Halloween was the best! We could wear our costumes to the restaurant and see many of our friends as they paraded up and down the aisles. How the service staff tolerated us, I will never know. It was truly a tribute to the sense of family. One Halloween, several years later, some friends and I had been attending a party at the Magic Castle in Hollywood and decided to finish the night at Canter's. We were all in costume and my costume was that of a 'car accident victim.'

I had great fun watching people get grossed out by my costume. One woman got up to call an ambulance but was intercepted before she made the call.

In our senior term at Fairfax High School, we had enough of school. A friend supplied some marijuana each morning for the walk to school and many times we just kept walking, past the school and down to Canter's. At that time, Sunset Blvd. was on fire with live rock and roll music, public drunkenness and "free sex" (not that I got any)! From Crescent Heights Boulevard, all the way west to Doheny Avenue, the Sunset Strip and the hippy generation was in full swing. So I guess our parents were right in keeping us away from there. We chose, instead to go to Canter's. It was our meeting place, our safety net of non-judgmental friends and service staff and a place of comfort where we could relax and seek refuge, any time we needed it.

I cannot express the gratitude and love I have for Canter's. It may sound odd, but Canter's was a critical, stable place in my life. If it were not there, at that time in my life, I doubt I would have survived. Now, I live several hundred miles away. When I do get to Los Angele, for whatever reason, I ALWAYS make it a point to stop for at least one meal and a whole lot of memories. The smells, the sounds, the welcoming staff and amazing food never fails to put me, and my guests (from all over the world), into a relaxed and happy mood. Thank you for continuing the tradition. It is wonderful to return to Canter's and find it unchanged and as welcoming as it always has been!"

Malinda

"It was 1976 and I was having my usual matzo brei and all of a sudden I felt a strange feeling in my stomach. I was going into labor! I managed to finish my entire meal and then my husband and I went home. Eight hours later we had a beautiful baby girl."

Cindy, age 70

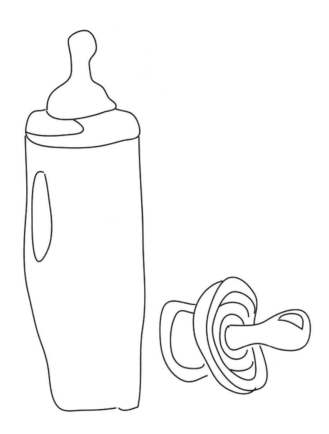

"1975: I was eating at Canter's around 2:00am when a tall blonde girl came in wearing a pink furry bikini...and wouldn't you know it, she stops at my table.

Me and my people were dumbfounded. The girl said she had a dead battery and wanted to know if we had cables. I didn't, but I told her I would use my Auto Club card to get her car started.

The Auto Club came. She gave me a joint and a big kiss. Turns out, it was Sandy West, drummer of The Runaways.

It could only happen at Canter's."

Bill, age 61

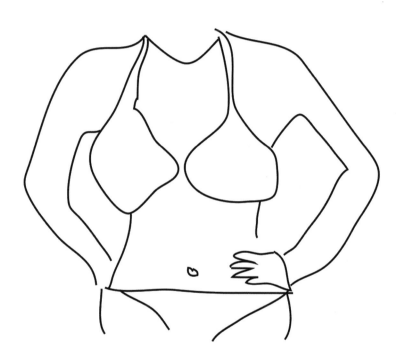

"My story begins in 1988 when at the age of fourteen, my family and I began frequenting Canter's. Canter's was always a place to grab a bite to eat after high school games, dances and other school functions. My four years of high school (88'-92') at Daniel Murphy Catholic High School were fantastic years filled with fantastic memories created at fantastic places, among those Sharky's Pizzeria & Arcade, Ed Debevic's, Aaron's Records, and of course Canter's Deli.

In April of 2000 I met the woman who would become my wife. Our third date took place at Canter's Deli. Little did I know that so many years later she would give birth to our only child in April 2015. When we drive back to the old neighborhood to visit my mom who still lives on Detroit Street all these years later, only two remnants of my precious youth remain: my mother's house and Canter's. My alma mater, Ed Debevic's, Sharky's, and Aaron's all closed their doors years ago.

Canter's is a direct tie to my cherished youth and a place where our precious Sophia can experience a big part of my life as a third generation Canter's patron.

Every visit to Canter's now is a memory-making moment for our family, particularly for our precious Sophia. Like Nona's house; Canter's is home."

Dax, age 44

"Late one night in the 1980s my wife Sarah and I were waiting to pay our check at the front of the restaurant. In through the front door bursts Rodney Dangerfield, with two gorgeous female escorts, one on each arm. He looked up, saw my wife, threw off the two women on his arms, staggered up and pointed at Sarah and said, "I want HER!!!"

Fortunately, Sarah declined his offer, and she is still here with me today."

Rick, age 63

"At Section 2 in the main dining area, my dad asked my mom to marry him. He hid the engagement ring in a black olive and before he could ask she almost swallowed the ring."

Ben

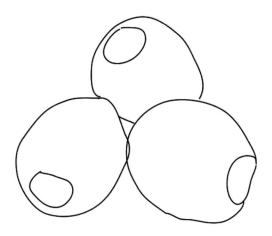

"My name is Richard Lodolo and I am ninety-two years old. I enlisted in the U.S Navy at age seventeen, right after I graduated from high school. I served aboard the USS Lake Champlain CV-39 (Atlantic) from 1943 to 1945. World War II, ended and I received an honorable discharge. When I returned home from the war, I took a flight to Long Beach (from the East Coast to West Coast). I then hailed a taxi and I asked the taxi driver to please 'Take me straight to Canter's!' It was the one in Boyle Heights. I ordered a bowl of matzah ball soup."

Richard, age 92

"In 1939, I was four years old. Your seating capacity was approximatley twenty people at the time. Eighty years later, this monthly treat is still alive."

Joe, age 84

Canter's Deli Brisket of Beef

1 cup ketchup

1 cup mustard

1/2 cup granulated garlic

1 teaspoon black pepper

1 (12-pound) brisket

5 carrots, peeled and sliced lengthwise

5 celery stalks

5 russet potatoes, peeled and quartered

5 yellow onions, chopped

5 garlic cloves, peeled

Preheat the oven to 350 degrees.

Mix together the ketchup, mustard, granulated garlic, and black pepper in a medium bowl, and rub into the beef. Place the beef in a roasting pan, add 1/3 of the vegetables to the pan, and fill it with 2 cups of water. Cover the pan with aluminum foil. Roast in the oven for 3 1/2 hours, or until the meat is browned and fork tender. About 1 hour before the brisket is done, add the potatoes and the remaining vegetables to the pan. For extra flavor, add the garlic. Cover again with the foil and continue roasting until it is done. Let the brisket rest for ten minutes so the juices do not run out, then slice it against the grain.

Serves 8 to 10

"1980: We rode up on a Harley and surprisingly got a parking space out front! I was with my friend Harry, who had just gotten a fresh tattoo and was dressed in all leather. Naomi was working the bakery that evening, and she looked terrified of us; the rough Rock and Rollers with the tattoos. I could see the tension (almost fear) in her eyes as we were choosing our pastries. But when Harry spoke to her in Yiddish...I will never forget the look on her face! All that fear was erased and she lit up like a bright light bulb with a huge smile and laughed. That moment stayed with me for years and was priceless. I think of it every time I come in here. RIP, sweet Naomi."

Audrey

"This was my first time here. I came with Nany and Grandma. I ordered a kid's hot dog, Caesar salad, and pink lemonade. I loved it all. You are so great Canter's."

Layla, age 8

"I was eleven-years-old and I was at Nibblers with my grandparents. My grandparents got into a huge fight because my grandfather wanted to come to Canter's. So, he paid for the meal at Nibblers and then we drove across town and ate a second meal at Canter's."

David, age 50

"Came here from Detroit in 1989. I was sitting at Canter's at 2:00am and the room started shaking. It was an earthquake! Everyone quickly exited except for me. I just sat and stared at the stained-glass ceiling, contemplating another bowl of matzah ball soup."

Sydney, Forever 21

Canter's

"We moved to the Fairfax district in 2012 and lived one hundred yards from Canter's Deli. We had breakfast here three times a week for two years. In 2014, we decided to move to a neighborhood that was more family-practical since we were pregnant with our first child. A few weeks before her due date, my wife and I decided on a whim to come back for a nostalgic breakfast at Canter's. Our son was born that night.

As I am writing this, I realize that we're back for breakfast and Ana Maria is eight and a half months pregnant again. If our son is born tonight, we're naming him Canter."

Tim & Anna Maria

"When my husband and I started dating back in 2015, we came to Canter's very late to have fries and milkshakes. When I saw steak fries on the menu, I thought it was literally fried pieces of steak. I got so excited! When the fries came out, I was so confused. I asked my husband 'Where's the steak?' He started laughing at me for confusing steak fries with fried steak. It's been an inside joke ever since!"

Lisette, age 25

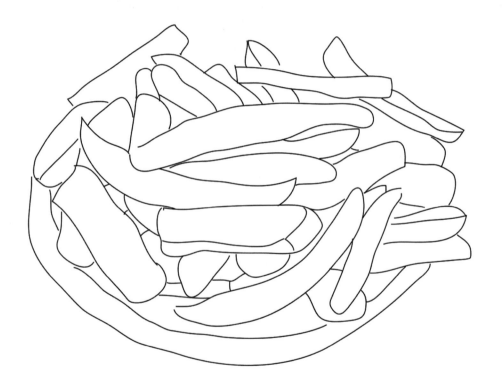

"My daughter and I lived a few blocks away for several years when she was a little girl. We would always get her a sprinkle cookie first while we waited for our food. For Mother's Day, she had bracelets made for us with the coordinates of Canter's. Our happy place."

Tania

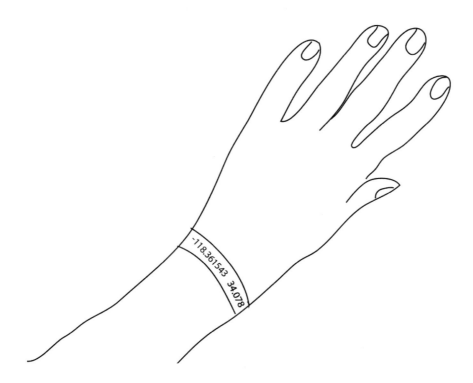

"I have too many Canter's memories to count so I'll just go with my most recent which was last night, so ravenous, with my dearest friends after our ten-year high school reunion. They all came in from across the country for an anticipated gathering but the late-night sandwich party was what we'll always remember: assessing how much, yet how little, we've changed—as existential Jews tend to do.

I never go to Canter's for the food and that's not a jab because I'm a lucky one who gets to sing there on Wednesday evenings to the drunken Fairfax dreamers. But Sunday nights man, they're what us Hollywood dreamers are made from... A melting pot of cultures draw in beneath the awning of a beloved Jewish home-for-all nestled in, where I deem to be, the heart of my hometown. Blaring through the dining room are the groaning guitar talents of strangers at an open mic night preceding Mr. Willie Chambers' midnight set. The amount of guitars glittering The Kibitz Room was a sight for my sore eyes. I peaked in as we were leaving, attempted to blend in with all the characters in the scene. Everybody is seen for who they are. I couldn't get to the exit without the bartender insisting he buy me a shot of Hunny Jack if only because he knows my name is Hunny and to let me know that I am always welcome. I love the Canter's family so much. They gave me this sanctuary to express my youth."

Hunny

"Every morning at 5 a.m., second generation owner Alan Canter arrives at the deli to meet with the produce truck. He personally handpicks every fruit and vegetable consumed in the restaurant. The colorful Fruit Cups filled with strawberries and chunks of melon and pineapple are not only his pride and joy, they symbolize Canter's dedication to quality"

— *(Beverly Hills Courier, Sep 9th 1994)*

"I went to Canter's at 3:00am on a Friday night. I had just finished a series of miserable finals at UCLA. What kept me going was the thought of Canter's hot pastrami sandwich after completing my post-exam nap. I always crave this place late at night—I'm in love with the history and the old Hollywood nostalgic vibes."

Mega, age 20

"My favorite TV show is *Girls* so naturally I'm a huge Lena Dunham fan. I remember a few years ago Lena posted an Instagram photo eating at Canter's Deli. Being the nerd I am, I went to Canter's that following Sunday and ordered exactly what she was eating in the photo; matzah ball soup, a side of bagel chips, and a Dr. Brown's cream soda. I enjoyed it so much! Thanks Lena for turning me on to an incredible place."

Kathy, age 27

"You know how, when you find that "special someone", it feels like you've discovered what you've been searching for your whole life? Well... that is your Belgian Waffle. It took traveling with my love, to a place we love, to find a waffle I love.

See, I had lost hope after an arduous search for a waffle that would live up to that first fluffy, flavorful, flakiness known as the Belgian Waffle. Finally, on our anniversary my wife and I crossed the entire country from Atlanta to LA. On our last night in a city that our hearts begged us to move to, we walked through the doors of Canter's. What happened next was a memory and a waffle to last a lifetime!"

Shaun, age 35

"About twelve years ago for Lent, I gave up chocolate. The night before Easter, we went to Canter's at about 11:00pm. I held on until midnight to have a Canter's chocolate cupcake with sprinkles. Only to my disappointment, someone had already bought all of them. The next day, I went to my aunt's house for Easter... she had bought all the cupcakes! It was a great day."

Karina

"I moved here from Santa Cruz in 1985 to a little $300 a month apartment on Spalding. I would walk over four to five times a week to eat at Canter's. I've never had a 'Jewish Deli' in my life until Canter's. I was in heaven. Trying to explain matzah ball soup to my mom on the phone was its own skit.

At that time, I befriended the wonderful, older, cantankerous, hilarious waitresses that ruled the roost here. I would ask them for advice on everything. They looked after me and I loved it. I have spent uncountable hours studying those autumn ceiling tiles. I love this amazing discovery in the heart of Los Angeles."

Thom, age 56

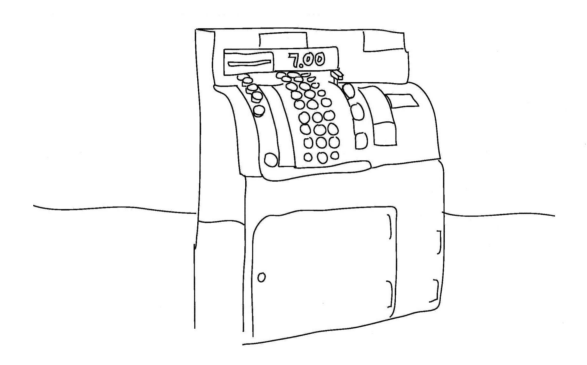

"Well, I have MANY GOOD memories of Canter's!!

Let me tell you...

I am shy of fifty-nine years old. I can remember coming to Canter's all my life! My parents and siblings would make the trip from the City of Lakewood often. Today it is sixty-one miles round trip and well worth it!! My Bubbie lived off Soto Avenue in Boyle Heights at the Jewish Home for the Aged. We would go visit her every week. To this day, when we pass her home, I can reminisce and smell that Bubbie smell! Her visit and Canter's were a big part of my growing up years.

When we would go to Canter's, I was always intimidated by the waitresses back then! Big, grey-haired, huge bosom ladies with New York accents! You better know what you were going to have because they didn't mess around! We usually ordered the same things; Matzah Ball soup, Kishka, Chopped Liver, Borsht soup and a Corned Beef sandwich! We ALWAYS brought dessert home. My all-time favorite cookie is "Keckle." It never gets old! Dad's favorite was poppy seed cake, Mom's was anything with apple, and my Papa loved the Halvah always at the register! It was fun to walk the block going in and out of the shops up and down Fairfax looking at all the tchotchkes and all the religious items.

Now moving forward...My husband and I have raised our three kids going to and loving Canter's just as much! As they have become young adults, they go on their own! Matzah ball soup, a sandwich and fries are their staple order. They always bring home lots of desserts to share! We have brought many family members here to eat. One of my favorite memories was just about five years ago. I set up a tour of Dodger Stadium and planned lunch for us after. There were eighteen of us so we had to sit upstairs (I say upstairs—three steps up!) I pointed out the picture of Shawn Green on the wall, my favorite Dodger player. I have his jersey, next to of course, Sandy Koufax's.

We were here on Saturday night, July 21, 2018. We brought our twenty-one-year-old daughter. She's home on summer break from college. We asked her where she wanted to go to dinner.... Without thinking about it, for sure it was Canter's!! Canter's will ALWAYS hold a SPECIAL place in my heart. I've enjoyed many bowls of soup, plates of food, lots of desserts and happy memories! It always smells the same when you walk in the door! A smell you love and don't forget!

I thank you for putting together a collection of Memories. I am sitting here with a big smile and a happy heart right now!! I think I will have another cup of coffee and enjoy a few of my Keckle cookies!!"

Michelle

"I, Jay Weiner, have been weaned on Canter's since I was born! In fact, my mother came to Canter's for potato salad in 1993 to serve at my Bar Mitzvah. Needless to say, I have spent a lot of time here. My grandpa, Solly Smolpnsky, has been a fresser at Canter's since the years at Boyle Heights. Fast forward and it is 2004 and grandpa Sol is ninety years old; almost ninety-one. Mind you he has never missed a meal at Canter's. When I say meal I mean half pastrami sandwich on rye, cup of barley bean soup, and a Dr. Brown's soda (cream or black cherry). Did I mention grandpa Sol is ninety, yes nienty years old and he ate like that. And of course, a few rugelach's compliments of Gary Canter aka 'Buddy Buddy.' After paying the bill, we always stopped at the deli for some cold cuts to go. And during the holidays we always got extra. My favorite times were kibitzing with 'Buddy Buddy.' To me, Gary was bigger than life and always full of energy. My favorite story is when he told me, 'Anytime you want, you just jump up on that efing ledge, reach your hand over, and help yourself to as many rugelach's as you want. And if someone has a problem, tell them to talk to me!' It's been over five years and I have yet to channel my inner chutzpah to jump up there and help myself.

Although grandpa and 'Buddy Buddy' are no longer with us, we still keep tradition alive. I miss that character and friend. May he rest in peace in the big bakery in the sky. "

Jay, age 38

"We had moved to Los Angeles so that I could attend law school. It was a difficult time for my little girl. She was lonely for her friends and her grandparents. She really just wanted to be home. Home was Bakersfield. Bakersfield was SO different from Los Angeles!

Summer was in 5th grade at the time and she—a tall, chunky, Caucasian girl—was the odd one out in her LA public school classroom. Her class consisted of all kinds of children with many languages and skin colors. Summer always had a hard time making friends.

One night while studying with my law school study group, we ended up at Canter's. I immediately knew it would be Summer's new favorite place in the world to eat! When I got home, I spared no detail in describing the beauty of your bakery counters and the things they held. Summer could not wait to go and experience Canter's for herself.

We did not have a lot of money in our budget for eating out in those days. It took 2 weeks of begging before I had the money to make our first trip to Canter's. I will never forget the look of sheer delight on Summer's face as she lit up with happiness when she saw all of those beautiful baked goodies. We had a lovely dinner that night and talked over her problems and worries.

We both relaxed for the first time in three months in LA. We took home dessert and pastries for breakfast the next morning. That easy, happy feeling from Canter's lasted for days. Her mood lightened from that day forward and we made Canter's a special stop whenever we were feeling stressed or sad.

As an adult, she took friends to Canter's and introduced them to the wonderful food and atmosphere. She LOVED doing this. As you may have noted, I'm writing of my girl in the past tense. She passed away on July 28, 2016 at the age of thirty-seven. She was a precious, sweet daughter and her love of Canter's was well known among her friends and family. I'll always remember the look on her face on that first visit when we walked into the door and she saw those cases of baked goods. I'll always be thankful to Canter's for that, especially now that I know how few years I'd have with her. Thanks for the good memories with my sweet girl."

Julie

Canter's Rock on Rye

The Kibitz Room serves up an eclectic menu of matzo and music

By David Wild

C OULD TONIGHT BE THE LAST Schmaltz?

Amid all the laughter and pastrami, there is an undeni-able feeling of nostalgia in the

Room – a tiny bar off to the side of the restaurant, with orange booths and lots of lowbrow ambience – has been the site of an unlikely hot new scene that's best de-scribed as Woodstock Meets the Borscht Belt. The Kibitz (the word is Yiddish for offering friendly advice or wisecracking) started out as an ultracasual jam session among a small gang of mostly twenty-

The Kibitz Room has since turned into a major L.A. draw. Slash of Guns n' Roses, Chris and Rich Robinson of the Black Crowes and members of Pearl Jam, Jellyfish and Mary's Danish have all been guest Kibitz jammers. Joni Mitchell, Johnny Depp, *Saturday Night Live*'s Mike Myers, singer-songwriter David Baerwald and the Red Hot Chili Peppers have

Many veterans of the first Kibitz jams are here early tonight, anxious to get their own bonding and playing in before the scene-making masses start sweeping in from Fairfax Avenue sometime before midnight. Most will be gone by the end of the night, when those who jam get to eat for free – only the musical director of the evening gets paid.

"I turned twenty-three last week, and here I am, talking about the [Cont. on 27]

imes performed a "People Get Ready"/"Crazy Love"/"The Weight" medley that has been one of the Kibitz Room's standards. "It's so pathetic," says Dylan, sitting in a booth with his girlfriend, Paige. "I sound like one of those old guys on *Cheers*. But in the beginning this place was *really* something fantastic and different."

Of course, how could a venue where one can hear "You Are My Sunshine," "Queen Jane Approximately" and "Hava Nageela" played on the same night not be a little fantastic and different? And certainly the L.A. music

Soon enough, the Kibitz Room along with Largo, a place across the street where TV actors once read poetry, and Damiano's, the best pizza joint in L.A. —

says Daniel Russell of the Freewheelers. "This is the way things are supposed to be." Like some others, Russell doesn't come around much anymore. "The whole thing got out of hand — out of *our* hands."

"Some girl came in one night and looked once and said, 'Is there another Kibitz that's, like, a club?' " says Jaffee with a chuckle. "And there are lots of people who come in wanting to know what the hell a 'kibitz' is. Maybe we should start a jamming chain nationwide."

"Anything that's really happening in this town

> "How could a venue where one can hear 'You Are My Sunshine,' 'Queen Jane Approximately' and 'Hava Nageela' played on the same night not be a little fantastic and different? And certainly the LA music scene was lacking something different."
>
> — *Rolling Stone Magazine*
> (on Canter's Kibitz Room)

lion bowls of chicken soup — a lot of them to rock legends. "Elvis would come in after playing the Pan Pacific," says Canter, who books the Kibitz Room. "The Beatles would come in after playing the Hollywood Bowl. Frank Zappa was in all the time. In the Sixties, you couldn't get into this place. All the hippies with munchies ended up here. Now we're full again with the hippies of the Nineties."

Rami Jaffee started Kibitzing at Canter's while attending Fairfax High School. "This is where I spent first period hiding out from the school security guards," says

om Retirement Hotel. "Oddly enough, Fairfax is turning into the Sunset Strip of the Nineties," says Andrew Slater, who manages the Wallflowers and plays guitar with his own band, the Kibitz regulars Ragged Glory. "Somehow it's actually become a cool place to be."

"It became a fun place to go in the City That Oversleeps," jokes Morty Coyle of the Imposters. "The real stars weren't the big names who dropped by but the guys who played all the time."

Observers of L.A.'s local musical culture — such as it is — spot a trend. "There

scene, as have some rock & roll decorating touches that irk some of the young old-timers. And yes, most of the Capitol A&R department is in attendance tonight. But if the Kibitz isn't quite the private musical clubhouse it once was, most of the veterans still talk fondly of their paradise lost.

"Whatever happens to our band or the other guys down the line," says Jakob Dylan, "I will always say that the coolest part was that one year when we were all hanging out in the Kibitz Room, making our record, just a bunch of pals playing 'The Weight' and 'My Girl' with a lot of heart and no in-

"1976: My buddy and I had ordered a big breakfast, only to discover we had no money. We told our waitress to hold our order because we had no cash. She frowned, looking concerned. 'Oh honey' she said. 'I can't afford a big breakfast, but I could help buy you a couple of English muffins and coffee.' We assured her that we just had forgotten our wallets and that we would be right back to eat in about an hour. We never forgot her kindness. Forty years later, my buddy and I still meet at Canter's."

Don, age 68

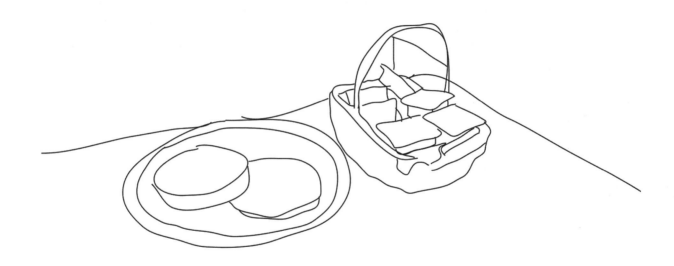

"My friends and I used to come here in the Eighties after a night of dancing and drinking at the discos. One night, we got here around 2:00am and while we were eating, I noticed Elliott Gould in a nearby booth. Because I had a little 'liquid courage' still in my system, I approached him and said, 'I never do this but could I please have your autograph?' He laughed and said, 'I probably always do this.' He then gave me his autograph on a napkin. I still have one layer of the napkin at home in a little baggy in my nightstand."

Taryn, age 50+

"It was my husband Ed who had introduced me to this legendary deli. Growing up in the Midwest I was not acquainted with genuine Jewish food or delis, and I loved all of it!

On July 27th, 1980, it was my thirty-second birthday. I was nine months pregnant with my first and only child, but I wanted to go out for my birthday. We went to the theater at the Music Center, then I requested a stop for a nosh at Canter's. I ordered borscht and thoroughly enjoyed every last drop.

We drove home to our little Venice apartment and within twelve hours, I was in labor and gave birth to my daughter Eden. Throughout her life, she has heard that her last meal 'in utero' was borscht at Canter's!"

Jenny, age 70

"A former New Yorker, I moved to LA in 1977 to rejoin the tonight show with Johnny Carson. I moved my mom here years later after my dad died. She had beginning stages of dementia. She lived on Hayworth and I would frequently pick her up and take her to Canter's to breakfast or lunch. Sometimes at lunch, we sat in the back room, which mom loved. As her dementia worsened, we continued coming here for breakfast and she insisted on sitting in the back room which was not open for breakfast, with some exceptions. I couldn't get her to understand that, so I asked the always wonderful Shirley, the hostess, if it were possible. Her response, 'When you reach your mom's age, you should have anything you want.'

Barbara

"I was raised on tortillas. My friend Teddy Schwall, a Puerto Rican Jew, brought me here for breakfast around 1970. I had my first toasted bagel with cream cheese and strawberry jam, loved it, and haven't stopped enjoying them since. Many years later, I returned for corned beef."

Tony, 73

"I first went to Canter's in the mid 60s. I would often visit at 2:00am when the Hollywood clubs closed. The picture on Canter's website for 1965 is exactly what it looked like. Funny after all this time everything about Canter's looks the same, even the waitresses. The food then was the best and it still is now.

The place was frequented by all the local music people. Originally called 'freaks', they later were called 'Hippies'. Almost daily, Canter's would see the exit of their regular patrons from the restaurant around 2:00am and the sidewalk would show throngs of long-haired boys and mini-skirted girls waiting to take their place.

Arriving late one night, I found that the police, who were rather notorious for harassing hippies at the time, had blocked the front doors of Canter's and had arrested everyone outside for 'blocking the sidewalk.' The lone hippie still there was 'Rodney, the Honorary Mayor of Hollywood.' Now, that era is looked back on with appreciation for all the famous and near-famous who went to Canter's each night after freaking out the rest of Hollywood. In a good way, I must say."

Joe

"We told each other we loved each other in Venice for the first time. We then went to Canter's and had bagel chips. If that's not romantic I don't know what is. I showed Taylor the magic of bagel chips like the good Jew I am."

Taylor and Grace

"My friend Nick and I were having lunch one day in 2002 when Gary Canter gave us a tour of the rarely-seen secret rooms upstairs where Marilyn Monroe and JFK allegedly had their rendezvous. Afterwards, Gary treated us to free rugelach!"

Jeff, age 57

Canter's Deli Marble Cake

3 cups sugar

1 tablespoon salt

3/4 teaspoon baking powder

2 tablespoons nonfat dry milk powder

2 1/2 cups cake flour

6 eggs

1 1/4 cup shortening

1 cup water

1/4 cup chocolate syrup

Preheat the oven to 350 degrees. Grease 2 loaf pans.

Using an electric mixer on medium speed, mix the sugar, salt, baking powder, milk powder, cake flour, eggs, and shortening. Add the water and mix for an additional 2 minutes on medium. Drizzle the chocolate syrup over the batter, then cut through the batter with a knife several times to give a marbled appearance. Bake for 35 to 40 minutes, until it is golden.

Serves 8 (2 loaves)

"We had been coming to Canter's for a year and a half and our favorite waittress was Candice. Finally, in August 2016 we looked across the table at each other and said 'It is time to get married.' We went and got our rings right after breakfast. Even now we try to come in every weekend and sit at our regular booth. We now start our mornings every weekend with Canter's favorites: Candice, Michael and Anna. It's great to see familiar friendly faces at a place we love."

Jake & Justin

"I was born in 1944, so I have a very LONG history with Canter's. I grew up in the Los Feliz area and when I was thirteen we moved to Beverly Hills. My two grandmas lived on streets on either side of Fairfax: Hayworth and Genesee. I ate at Canter's regularly—probably since 1949. Every Saturday my Nanny would take me and my two cousins to lunch at Canter's after my ballet class, which was across the street from Nate 'n Al's Deli. But Canter's was so much better! Then we'd go to the movies on Hollywood Boulevard.

Fast forward to the 60s when I was a hippie and would sing and panhandle with my boyfriend out front on the sidewalk on the weekend nights around midnight or 2:00am. Then we'd go inside to eat with celebs: rock musicians like the Doors and movie stars like Sal Mineo. My favorite story is the night I had three waitresses offering to help me find my 'contact lens' that had fallen under the table, but it wasn't really a contact lens—it was a hit of LSD!

In the early 70s I went to work for a phone company in West Hollywood and retired after twenty-five years. I was the second female phone installer in Southern California. I ate lunch at Canter's at least a couple times a week. One Sunday in the 80s, my daughter took the train from San Diego to Santa Barbara to visit her friend at college. On her way back to San Diego, she craved a corned beef sandwich from Canter's. I got it for her and literally handed it through the window of the train at LA's Union Station downtown.

I hate to admit that two of my five wedding cakes came from Canter's.

I live in Arizona now but go back to LA often to visit family and friends. Last year I actually had brunch with a friend at Canter's, went for a walk around the neighborhood, and then met another friend for lunch there!

My favorite meal: A Downtowner with hot pastrami & swiss cheese on a Kaiser roll, dry—no mustard, and new pickles. Dr. Brown's cream soda, and a black & white cookie for dessert."

Pam

"There are many secret places that people can go to have parties and discuss business in this restaurant. They are in corners of this place. Ten people might be sitting in a corner and you would never be able to see them."

Laurie, age 60

"My Polish Jewish grandma, Sally, lived a few blocks away from Canter's. She would take me for errands on Fairfax. We would stop at the market for white fish, then Merlo's Meats, then Canter's for soup. This was our regular routine. Always a stop at the bakery for bagels and of course rum cake. Always the rum cake."

Marcia, age 63

"After a week spent at Disneyland, on our last day of vacation, my sister and I bought a huge duffle bag and went to Canter's for sandwiches. After eating our two sandwiches, we ordered another dozen sandwiches and a jar of pickles. We also stopped at the bakery on the way out. We filled up the duffle bag and headed for LAX. As we walked to our gate with our prized possessions for the short flight back to San Francisco, we saw more than one security dog turn their head and follow us with their noses. We thought for sure that we were going to get stopped and searched and our duffle bag seized as contraband. Love Canter's!"

William

"My grandfather came over from Russia more than one-hundred years ago. He got here with nothing and did not speak a word of English. He worked hard to get his siblings out as well. He met my grandmother who had recently arrived from Hungary, also with nothing but her desire for a better life. They both worked hard, learned to speak fluent English and became US citizens as soon as they could and got good jobs. He was a butcher and also earned extra money as a boxer and wrestler. She became a bank secretary and then an administrator. Together they opened a kosher market in Kansas City.

When my grandparents became too old to deal with the harsh Kansas City winters in the early 60s, they sold the market and moved to Los Angeles. Their 'La Brea' apartment was less than a mile from Canter's!!

My grandfather worked as a butcher at the Farmer's Market and my grandmother worked at a local bank. When I was growing up in Orange County, I'd frequently visit and stay with them in LA off and on throughout the 60s. I cannot tell you how many times I walked to Canter's for breakfast, lunch, dinner, or just a nosh. It was a tradition. It felt like home.

Since that time, I have had the good fortune to travel extensively both in the Air Force and as an international airline pilot. Number one always on my list when visiting a new city—find the best Jewish Deli in town! I've found some great ones especially in cities like New York, DC, Rome,

San Francisco, Madrid, Philly, and even San Diego. But none have ever replaced the feeling, the tastes, the atmosphere, of home... I mean Canter's.

Mike

"When I was a child my father brought me to Canter's and introduced to me what his father had introduced to him. He ordered for us both— as he wanted his favorite memory to become my favorite memory. We had the corned beef sandwich on rye with a dill pickle on the side. Also a chocolate phosphate to wash it down. I had never had either, and they both became some of my favorite dishes of all time. Every time he brought me back, we had the same meal together and he would just sit there and watch me smile.

I now have a four-year-old son, and I plan on bringing him to Canter's and sharing that same memory with him. This is becoming a family tradition that can be treasured down the line."

Paul

"The memory is this: when our daughter Oona was an infant we used to come to Canter's because there was a nice hum that tended to cancel out our child's crying so we could eat in peace. On a particular day Oona was crying, the waitress leaned over and said, 'give her a pickle.' My wife and I exchanged glances and said, 'Not happening!'' Oona kept crying and this time a different waitress popped by and said, 'Give her a pickle.' At this point I did just that and Oona quieted down and enjoyed the pickle! As parents, we learned something at Canter's."

Steve, age 69

Restaurant REVIEW

Canter's
by Shirley Firestone

I read that Canter's was voted #1 for pastrami by the *L.A. Times*, so when my friend said he wanted a big, thick, fat pastrami sandwich with lots of pickles, that's where we went. For those readers that can remember as far back as when Canter's was on Brooklyn Avenue in Boyle Heights, you will probably choke up with nostalgia thinking about the two hot dogs for a nickel. One came in a bun and the other was put in your hand. Mile-high corned beef, pastrami, tongue and meats were 10 cents, loaded with favorite embellishments all stuffed between two pieces of thick rye bread and salami sandwiches three inches tall were priced at a nickel. That was about 70 years ago, they're still a one family business.

They've fed the likes of legendary Eddie Canter, Danny Thomas and Billy Gray of "Band Box" fame (goes back to World War II). The family is proud to tell people that Academy Award nominated actor Nicholas Cage met his wife Patricia Arquette in their dining area and other notables who made Canter's their home away from home have included Marilyn Monroe and Arthur Miller, Cary

vegetable, plus potato, bread and butter and dessert of jello, sherbet or ice cream with coffee or tea. Choices include a half roasted, barbecued, boiled or broiled chicken, roast brisket of beef and a whole slew of items like meatloaf with mashed potatoes, hot corned beef and cabbage, liver and onions, stuffed kishka, roast tongue, also turkey with stuffing and more. Each are served with embellishments.

A beacon for deli lovers

When writing about a deli I don't refer to my particular choices because a Jewish deli is a Jewish deli, and everyone knows what they serve. I've always thought that favorite ones

doughy ones. Either way it's still knish! So, you choose the place tha does it your way.

Many deli eaters love the hub of th familiar sounds and aromas. And i many cases one can depend on le than desirable service that's either to fast, slow or indifferent; all for the j of divine scents coming from herrin corned beef, salami, pastrami, fanta tic pickles and fish platters.

Breakfast is served every day aroun the clock, with a special deal costir $6.50 from 6 to 11 a.m. However yc can still get Matzo Brey, lox with eg; and onions, Benedict or Florentin Belgian waffles and all the famili breakfast items priced under $1 (and much less).

I love looking at the bagels, bread cheesecakes, turnovers, French pa tries, coffee cakes, Napoleons ar éclairs in the display cases upon ente ing. My favorite is their mondel brea the Jewish answer to Italy's biscot And at Canter's the old-fashione soda fountain menu has me saliva ing over banana splits, root beer floa malts, shakes and sodas.

It's interesting to note that over tl years, Canter's sold over two millic pounds of lox; three million poun of potato salad; nine million poun of corned beef; 10 million mat balls; 20 million bagels and 24 m lion bowls of chicken soup (Jewi penicillin).

They do an excellent job on par planning and have a special cateri department. You can call for pric They're open 24 hours offering

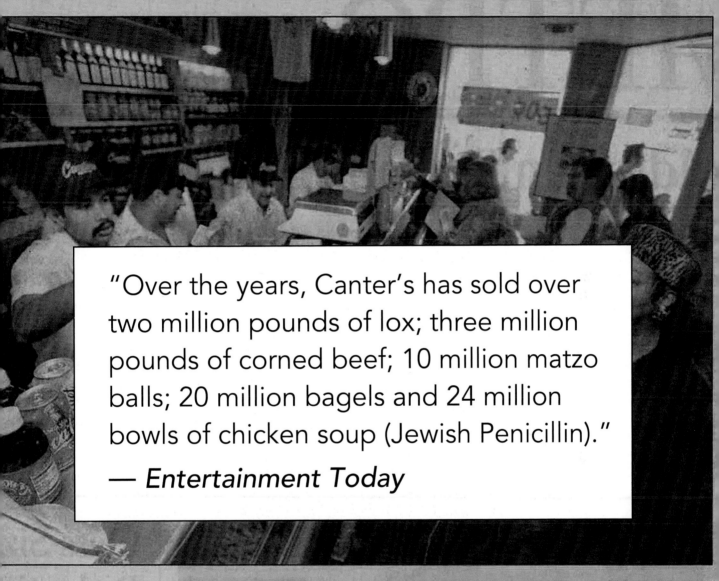

"Over the years, Canter's has sold over two million pounds of lox; three million pounds of corned beef; 10 million matzo balls; 20 million bagels and 24 million bowls of chicken soup (Jewish Penicillin)."

— *Entertainment Today*

A 50-Cent Milestone

atrons like Meyer Levy, center, and Deborah
homas, behind him, flock to Canter's deli as the
airfax district restaurant celebrates its 50th

"1991ish...It was a Monday night. Johnny Depp walked up to my table and asked for a bite of my potato pancakes... I happily obliged."

Lonna

"My employees know I love Canter's...they also know that if I have a meeting within fifteen minutes of Canter's I'm going to bring them back a two-pound box of cookies. Love 'em!"

John

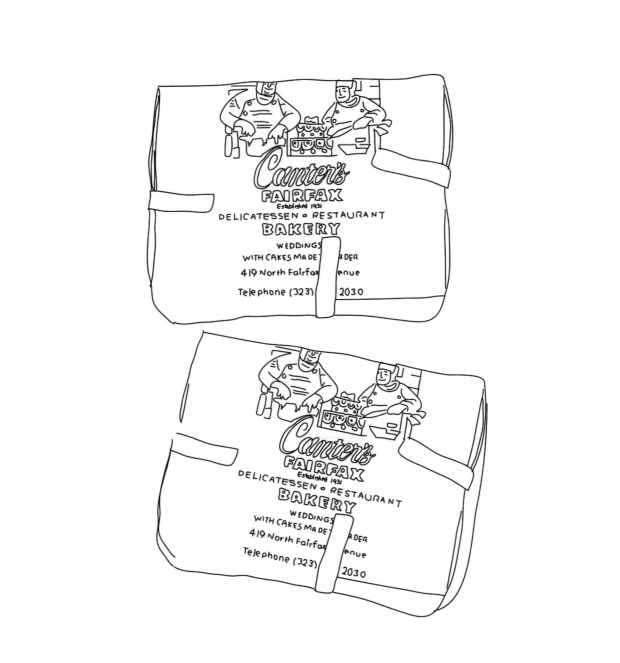

"The inseparable bond that my uncle Gary Canter and I formed mostly took place at Canter's Deli. Canter's was absolutely Gary's pride and joy! He especially had pride in his grandparents, Ben and Jenny (the founders), to the point where it was unwavering. Gary had the best sense of humor of anyone that ever lived. Being with him was the definition of entertainment. I enjoyed sitting with him in the Kibitz Room for hours talking about everything and anything. And the hand-cut pastrami sandwiches were just a little bonus as they were the best sandwiches I ever had in my life. He made them for me the exact same way his grandfather made them for him. Gary was always experimenting with food until it was the perfect version of itself. Nobody took food more seriously than he did and he really knew what he was doing!"

Josh, age 22

"My parents would stop every summer going back to San Francisco loading up on bagels and lox. Fast forward to 1972, I took my girlfriend, now wife, to Canter's on the way to Mexico in my VW bus. We ordered corned beef sandwiches. As the deli man was making our meal, she asked for mayo on the bread. The deli man asked if she were a 'Goy' and told her no one puts mayo on their sandwich. Now that I am older, I have become a mule to my friend in Northern California, bringing them Canter's food for all to enjoy."

Steve, age 65

"I moved to LA in the 1980s. My family had little to no experience with Jewish delis up 'til then, so, I was pleased to introduce Canter's, my new favorite spot, to my mom when she would visit from New Mexico. Matzoh ball soup, knishes, bagels—she loved it all, just like me.

But her love of Canter's was reinvented on the day she ordered a beautiful slice of cheesecake. She dug in, and to my surprise, decided it wasn't what she hoped for. Nice, but different. I summoned the waitress, against mom's shy protests, to see what we might order as an alternate. She listened, called mom 'sweetie', and brought us exactly the kind of cheesecake that took mom over the moon, all for no extra charge and with a big smile. We left with a box full of pastries which fueled us over the next few days, and from then on, any of mom's visits always had to start with a visit to Canter's, without exception. Now all of our family back home aspires to experience Canter's, and one by one, they do."

Shannon, age 54

"Back in my formative years I was engaging in my weekly Tuesday ritual of consuming an entire sky-high, potato salad and a whole plate of pickles. I had just placed my order at the counter and was casually reading the newspaper when someone sat down to my left and started studying the menu.

The waiter swung by with my pickles a few minutes later and asked the man for his order. He replied, in a most imperious tone of voice, 'I'd like a turkey and swiss on white bread with extra mayo.' Realizing the massive shande that was transpiring right next to me, I promptly slammed down my newspaper and exclaimed 'You make me sick sir! How can you defile the fifth holiest site in Judaism with such an order?'

At this point, Gary Canter was coming around the corner laughing at what was transpiring at his counter. The people in the booth behind me began applauding my courageous act.

The flummoxed customer, to his great credit, changed his order to corned beef on rye and the Jewish people were saved from yet another tragedy."

Nathan

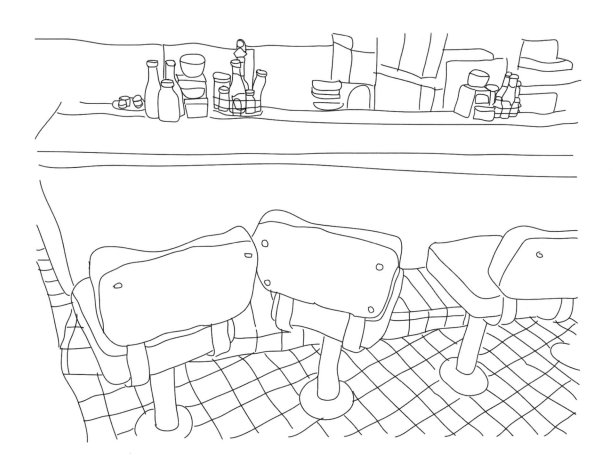

"I come from a dysfunctional family. My friends in my teen years knew I loved Hollywood and especially Canter's. They would surprise me with trips out to Canter's when they knew it was a hard time for me at home. They didn't care about the hour-plus drive or that I had money to eat— they treated every time. These trips had such an impact on me, my well-being, and a moral booster for such a fragile teen. Thank you for allowing me the chance to share."

Miranda

"When I was nineteen years old, my buddies and I left the Palladium where we had just witnessed one of the best concerts ever. AFI opened up, and Rancid closed it out. My forehead beaded with sweat as the crowd pushed and shoved their way around the large music hall. Despite my youth, two hours of running around slamming into a thousand grown sweaty men, I had to succumb to my massive thirst. As I approached the bar, I reached for my wallet and with a slap to my right buttock a faint denim poof resounded over the aggressive shouts of misfit anthems. My heart sank and panic set in. My wallet was gone, along with $20, my driver's license, and my punch card to my favorite frozen yogurt spot. After the panic came frustration as I surveyed the floor for a glimpse of a brown leather wallet. I felt lost, naked, taken advantage of and ready to fight the next suspect walking out of the show with a smile on his face.

My night was ruined and at the time, my nineteen-year-old life. As I met up with my two buddies, I vented my frustration. I explained that I wanted out, and wanted to go home. They said, 'Hey man, we are hungry and want to go to Canter's' which made me even more mad. How could they be hungry as my world was falling down all around me. We soon made a right out the of the venue, cruised down Sunset, and hung a left on Fairfax to Canter's, where all the people seemed to be living it up! My friend Chris said 'Hey! Snap out of it, you coming in?' 'No, I'm not coming in' as the vintage Canter's sign lit and reflected off the hood of the car. After punching the backseat for a minute, I got out of the car, slammed the door, and sat on the concrete sidewalk just outside Canter's. As I put my head into my hands, an elderly black man walked beside me, pulled out his blanket, shoved his possession of garbage he had collected for the day into the corner, and calmly rested for the night. He was doing all he could do to survive. At the risk of being rude, I stared at him, reflected on my life, took a deep breath, got up and walked into Canter's to join my friends.

I learned three things that night. Canter's has the best pie in the world, the best staff, and always put your wallet in your front pocket at concerts. I realized my life wasn't that bad and things could always be worse."

Eliseo, age 38

"1995:My then roommate and I were both Los Angeles natives. We were, at the time, dating two friends who were Marines stationed at Pendleton, but from smaller towns on the East Coast. One night we all went to Canter's after a late movie. One of the Marines sees someone in the corner booth, next to the stairs to the bathroom. He gets wide-eyed and says, 'Holy s***, that's Christian Slater over there!'

The other guy whips his head around to look and gets similarly excited. But we just glance casually and say, 'Oh, yeah, that happens.'

'I can't believe how blasé you are about this! That's just sad!' exclaims one of our beaus.

'Well, you grow up here, and you see them all the time, I guess. You get to realize they're real people,' I respond, and my roommate nods her full agreement. A little later, my roommate gets up to go to the bathroom. While going up the stairs, she trips and nearly falls flat on her face. The next morning, she bemoans, 'I can't believe I tripped and fell right in front of CHRISTIAN SLATER!'

I guess we're not as blasé as we thought we were!"

Monica

"This is about my father, Bernard Horn. We celebrated my father's seventy-fifth birthday at Canter's in February 2013. I moved to Los Angeles in 2008 to go to USC. Whenever my dad visited me, we would go to Canter's, and he would reminisce about when he attended USC in the 1950s. He has grown up at Canter's with his mother and grandparents (who lived nearby on Sycamore Avenue.) So, given how much those Canter's memories meant to my father and me, it felt appropriate to have his 75th birthday party there. It was a surprise birthday party—and even though we had hosted surprise parties for his sixtieth, sixty-fifth, and seventieth birthdays, he still had NO IDEA we were throwing a surprise party for him.

When he hobbled up the stairs and saw his friends and family waiting for him, he was shocked. It was a great night. In lieu of a birthday cake, we ordered seventy-five rugelach (or "arugula" as he sometimes called them) and put a candle on top. I gifted him with a tin collection box from the Jewish National Fund. (When I was growing up, before starting a load of laundry, he would walk around the house with a laundry basket, saying 'Please help the Jewish National Fund.') We also planted a celebratory birthday tree in Israel in honor of 'Nicely Nicely Bernard,' as he liked to call himself.

A few days after the party, he sent an email to my siblings, my mom, and I, recapping the night:

We went to Canter's (number uno LA Deli) for dinner and low and behold, twenty people or so were waiting with a happy birthday surprise. How Shirley [my mom] does this every five years is beyond me but once again, I was in the dark. A real nice and touching time for me.

My dad died a year later, on November 7, 2014, at age seventy-six. My siblings and a few close family members flew to Los Angeles immediately following his passing. In lieu of an immediate funeral, we opted to hold a celebration of life at a later date. But we did do one thing to honor him that November weekend: we all went to Canter's, and enjoyed (lean) corned beef on rye and Dr. Brown's Diet Cherry."

Rachel

"My mother used to LOVE to come to Canter's! Her favorite was the barley bean soup. Whatever she ordered, she started with the barley bean soup. Mom had a stroke in 1999 and I continued to bring her to Canter's. She could never decide what she wanted to eat, so I would always order the barley bean soup and she always enjoyed each bowl as if it were the first time she had it.

After Mom passed, it was hard to go to Canter's but one day, I went. So many memories, it was sad but I had a bowl of barley bean soup in memory of Mom. I felt she was there with me, enjoying the soup as much as I was. Now, I come often to enjoy the great food and for the memories."

Lawanda

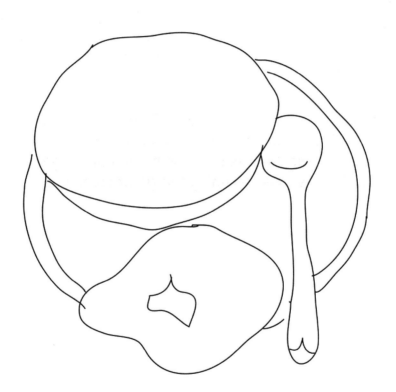

"The first time I stepped into Canter's Deli was in March of 2006. Canter's was offering a corned beef sandwich special for $0.75 in honor of their 75th anniversary. I remember reading about it in a local newspaper. I immediately fell in love with the whole throwback vibe and of course delicious food. After my first corned beef sandwich I was hooked. My husband and I make the drive from Long Beach often. We have been customers for twelve years now. So many happy memories here!"

Jenny, age 34

Canter's
RESTAURANT
BAKERY
DELICATESSEN

419 N. Fairfax.

Come Celebrate our 75th Anniversary with a

75¢ Hot Corned Beef

World Famous 24 Hour Restaurant • Deli • Bakery • Bar

CANTER BROS
DELICATESSEN

1931   (323) 651-2030   2006

"I went to Canter's almost nightly as a teen in the 1980s. I can remember when we could still smoke in there! We were Goth girls going in at 2:00am after the clubs. Meeting and seeing stars right next to our friends. David Lee Roth was in almost nightly with at least three girls wearing 'nothing.' I got to meet Sean Penn there in the parking lot. He was a dream and SO nice.

One night I was up front and a big limo drives up and Rodney Dangerfield walked in to pick his order up in the nicest suit I have ever seen. I almost passed out!!!

I live a bit far now and I am dreaming of a potato knish and a pickle! The staff was always so kind to us kids and put up with everything. One year an older waitress made my roommate and I homemade fudge for the holiday and it touched me so very deeply. Part of me grew up there and it always felt like home. "

Christine

"My father passed away suddenly in 1977 when I was only seven years old. He was an only child, so visiting my grandparents —who lived in the Fairfax area—became all the more important for them as they yearned to cling to the only human connection they still had to their departed son, that being my sister and me. A few years later my grandmother passed away, the exact medical reason I can't precisely recount, but undoubtedly the real underlying reason was from her broken heart. As time passed and we grew older, we would visit my grandfather and, once he was no longer able to drive himself, we would pick him up and go out to lunch or dinner. Canter's was a staple destination for the good part of the final twenty years my sister and I spent with our grandfather.

Walking into Canter's and inhaling the aromas that filled the low-slung bakery and deli counter areas in the front of the restaurant was the first indelible greeting Canter's offered its guests. One's senses were further titillated upon observing the visual majesty of the seating area of the restaurant as it opened up to boast one of the most special and unique ceilings west of the Sistine Chapel: a tapestry of maple tree canopy photographs, repeatedly displayed across the expanse and back-lit to accentuate the pure artistry of the feature. Settling into a pleather booth and surveying the Formica wood-grain table-top adorned with its standard array of salt and pepper, sweeteners, mustards and jams, it was rarely long before we would be greeted by one of the many long-standing waitresses who so well-represented Canter's. Then came what was usually the most demanding dilemma of the visit: making a decision on what to order. The food at Canter's rarely disappointed and inevitably we would find ourselves shuffling up to the cashier, our bellies full of high-calorie meals, yet not so stuffed that we wouldn't spend time surveying the Joyva Jelly and Halvah bars, mints, gum and other goodies that would solicit our interest before stepping back out onto the brightly sunlit Fairfax sidewalk.

My grandfather has long passed but I still frequent Canter's with other family and friends when the opportunity presents itself. Canter's doesn't hold a specific memory for me as much as Canter's is a place of memories. Visiting Canter's brings those memories rushing back in all their vivid splendor, and I pray I will have the ability to re-live those memories, and create new ones, for many years to come."

Corey

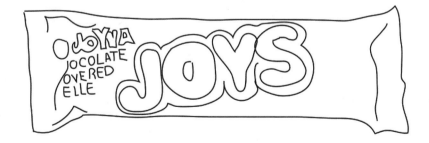

"In summer 2016 I got to see one of the greatest bands in the world perform two sold-out nights in a row at Dodger Stadium (one of the greatest baseball stadiums in the world!) That favorite band of mine is Guns N' Roses! Los Angeles rock and roll heroes! After the concert had let out I needed to refuel as singing along for three hours in that huge crowd had really wore me out. Thankfully I knew of a place not far from home where I could get a good meal late at night. That place was Canter's!

I walked by the famous Guns N' Roses booth and stood there for a moment thinking how amazing it is that a local band could create such a buzz and take the music world by storm to a point where they eventually became the most dangerous band on the planet. Two decades later Axl, Slash and Duff were back. A big part of their early story began at Canter's... here was this booth, nearly identical to how it looked when their first band photo was taken in it thirty years prior."

Louie

"In 1931, my father started a business in Boyle Heights on Brooklyn Avenue. It was called the United Dairy Store, and he put a large butter churn in the store front window where he gave free buttermilk in little paper cones to anyone who wanted it.

When my mother would go to the store on Saturday to visit and to help out, she would take my two older brothers and me to Canter Bros. Delicatessen for lunch. What a treat! I can still remember those corned beef sandwiches and how my brothers and I looked forward to devouring them. Also, when I think of Canter's, that wonderful smell of freshly baked rye bread, pastries, corned beef and pickles gets my saliva glands working and then I must go and get my fix.

I am now ninety-nine years old and have been going to Canter's for eight decades and enjoying the food more and more."

Lillian, age 99

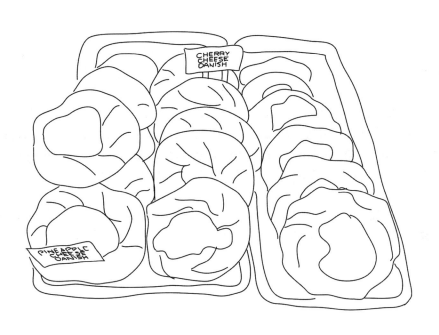

BILLY GRAY'S BAND BOX SPECIAL	FISHERMAN'S FOLLY	CANTER'S FAIRFAX	BEVERLY THREE-DECKER
Open Face Chopped Liver & Chopped Egg	Whitefish, Cream Cheese & Bermuda Onion	Chicago Pastrami and Hot Corned Beef	Turkey, Tongue, Pastrami Cole Slaw & Canter's Dressing
.75	.75	.75	.95

1955

CANTER'S ORIGINAL SPECIAL
One Sandwich Not enough? Two - too many!!
Try One and One Half and You won't leave any

MIDNIGHT SPECIAL
CHARCOAL BROILED STEAK SANDWICH
With Tomato and Lettuce
French Fries • Cole Slaw

.95

BUCK BENNY
Grilled Frankfurter
with Pickle and Sauerkraut

.35

CANTER BURGER
HAMBURGER DeLUXE
with Tomato, Lettuce
Onion & Canter's Dressing
Potato Chips

.50

with Cheese 10¢ Extra

EPPIS ESSEN . . . SANDWICHES

TURKEY	.75
ROAST BEEF	.65
CANTER'S HOT CORNED BEEF	.50
SALAMI & EGG	.60
HOT CHICAGO PASTRAMI	.50
PICKLED TONGUE	.45
PEPPERED MEAT	.50
CHICAGO SALAMI	.40
CHICAGO BOLOGNA	.40
SMOKED LIVERWURST	.35
CHOPPED EGG	.35
CHICAGO ROLLED BEEF	.50
TUNA SALAD	.35
CHICKEN SALAD	.35
CHOPPED LIVER	.45
SMOKED SALMON (LOX)	.45
SWISS CHEESE	.40
CREAM CHEESE	.30
JACK CHEESE	.30
AMERICAN CHEESE	.30
HAMBURGER SANDWICH	.50
CHEESEBURGER	.60

SOUPS
Served with Crackers

SOUP DU JOUR	.20
CABBAGE BORSCHT	.20
COLD BEET BORSCHT	.25

APPETIZERS

IMPORTED ANCHOVIES, LETTUCE, TOMATO AND SLICED ONIONS	.70
SMOKED SALMON (LOX)	.55
HOMEMADE PICKLED HERRING	.45
SCHMALTZ HERRING	.45
CHOPPED HERRING	.40
CHOPPED LIVER	.50
SLICED SALAMI	.40
FRUIT COCKTAIL	.20
GEFILTE FISH	.50
CHOPPED EGG	.40

CHILLED SALADS

TUNA OR SALMON SALAD	.90
IMPORTED SARDINE SALAD	.95
CHICKEN SALAD DE LUXE	.90
WHITE FISH, LETTUCE, COLE SLAW & POTATO SALAD	1.45
DAIRY SALAD—LOX, SARDINES, AMERICAN CHEESE, POTATO SALAD AND COLE SLAW	.95
SMOKED KIPPERED COD WITH SALAD	.95

LITTLE NEW YORKER	BIG NEW YORKER	O'MALLEY	DANNY THOM...
Lox and Cream Cheese, on a Bagle	Lox and Cream Cheese On a Kaiser or Onion Roll	Canter's Hot Corned Beef or Pastrami, Sliced Tomatoes & Canter's Dressing	HOT SALAMI on Rye B.. Cole Slaw & Pickle
.40	.55	.60	.55

Open 24 Hours Daily Except
Monday Until 1 A.M.

EGGS and OMELETTES

DELICATESSEN OMELETTE	.75
CORNED BEEF & EGGS	.85
PASTRAMI & EGGS	.85
CHICAGO SALAMI AND EGGS	.70
FRANKFURTER AND EGGS	.75
LOX AND SCRAMBLED EGGS	.75
LOX, EGGS AND ONIONS	.85
EGGS AND ONIONS	.65
TWO EGGS, ANY STYLE	.50
CHEESE OMELETTE	.65

RELISHES and SIDE DISHES

FRENCH FRIES	.20
SLICED RED TOMATOES	.25
POTATO SALAD	.15
BAKED BEANS	.15
APPLE SAUCE	.15
COLE SLAW	.15
KOSHER DILL PICKLES OR TOMATOES	.15
SWEET PICKLES	.15
SAUERKRAUT (EASTERN)	.15
GREEK OLIVES	.20
KISHKA	.45
SLICED RED TOMATOES, LETTUCE & CANTER'S DRESSING	.40

CHEESE PLATE

FOUNTAIN

ICE CREAM	.15
COCA COLA	.15
SUNDAES	.35
SODAS	.30
MALTS	.35
GIANT BANANA SPLIT	.50
CHOCOLATE PHOSPHATE	.15
CHERRY PHOSPHATE	.15
ROOT BEER FLOAT	.30

DESSERTS

HOMEMADE CREAM CHEESE CAKE	.25
ASSORTED DANISH PASTRY	.15
FRUIT CUP	.20
STEWED PRUNES	.15
CAKES	.20
FRUIT PIES, PER CUT	.20
CREAM PIES	.25
FRUIT TARTS	.25
JELLO WITH CREAM	.20
ICE CREAM	.15
MELON IN SEASON	.25
BAKED APPLE	.25
WITH CREAM	.10 EXTRA

BEVERAGES

COFFEE	.10
HOT TEA	.10
MILK (Individual Containers)	.15
SKIM MILK	.10

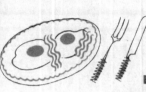

"In 1994, about a year after my husband passed away at the young age of fifty-four, my children nudged me to start dating or at least get out of the house. A dear friend Debbie, who also lost her husband one month after mine, and I were commissioned to go to a jewish singles dance in L.A. We did with much anxiety and apprehension and, low and behold, I was danced away into the arms of a lovely gentleman named Harry. Long story short, we dated and had our first meal together at this wonderful establishment. Harry lived in West Hollywood and I loved deli food so we met at Canter's. Harry, a child survivor of the Holocaust, was very comfortable with wholesome food rather than a posh place with silver and crystal. When he passed away in 2015, we celebrated his eighty-seven-year life at—you guessed it—your home. Twenty years of memories and a little heartburn!"

Faith

"Canter's flows in my blood, in the nicest possible sense. I have been visiting since I was five years old and my first vivid memory is passing slices of fresh rye bread across our ivy-covered fence to our neighbor, Tess. I treasure the many family get-togethers we had in the booths, being seated by a smiling hostess with short reddish hair. We would order a full turkey dinner or a piled-high corned beef sandwich with deli mustard on rye with a pickle on the side. We would pick up the legendary rum cake and those tasty macarons for Passover. I even celebrated my Bar Mitzvah luncheon on the second-floor reception room.

I am now sixty-nine years old and have known most of the deli crew by their first names for many years—patriarchal gray-haired George, Roberto, Manny, et al. The deli crew would always greet me with a warm 'Hello, doc', and they knew that I had a penchant for picking the deli end pieces ('Wrap them up as is; no slicing required.'). They would even go back into the kitchen before the morning Matzoh ball soup was ready to fill my order/desire.

I remember Alan Canter early in the morning as he was preparing food at the deli counter. My friends and I would often stop by at night for a large plate of French fries with ketchup, especially after a movie or a Fairfax High football game. The mural on the wall in the parking lot has always been a thing of beauty, chronicling the original Canter's in Boyle Heights as well as a lovely panorama of Los Angeles Judaica. I think Sandy Koufax is included. Even though I moved out of the Fairfax district long after college (and have sampled Brent's, Langer's, Jerry's, and others since then), I still find my way to Canter's whenever I am in the area...my Aliyah. Like I said: Canter's flows in my blood. I pray they go on for many more years to come."

Henry

"For Natalie and I, Canter's has become a favorite tradition. We absolutely love coming to Canter's after Dodger games. As a matter of fact, there has not been a single game that we have attended that was not later followed by a late-night meal at Canter's. Whether the team wins or loses, we can always count on this special place to end our night on a high note. Honestly, my sister and I could not imagine a night out at a Dodger game without Canter's afterwards."

Natalie & Matthew

"My greatest memory is from right now...Queen Latifah just walked into Canter's. THE QUEEN IS IN THE HOUSE."

Abby, age 18

"Eating Matzo Brei with my mother the night before Yom Kippur (Kol Nidre). She said I reminded her of her grandmother, and she began to cry. We hugged in the booth, then left for synagogue."

Ruby, age 16

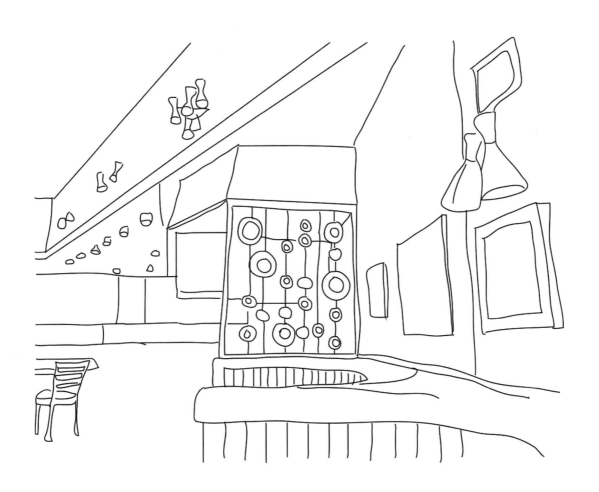

"Like the Deli, my family's Canter's story is also multigenerational. My father, Gilbert Morales, was born in Los Angeles and grew up in Lincoln Heights next door to Boyle Heights. As a boy, he worked for a relative who had a clothing store and would often be sent to Canter's on Brooklyn Avenue to pick up sandwiches. His love for Canter's was set from then on.

When he married my mom, my sister and I came along. He shared his love for Canter's with us and we too became fans. By that time, the deli had moved to its present location. As a child growing up in East LA, I thought it was normal to travel crosstown to Canter's on Fairfax. It was a drive but the sandwiches and soups were so good and you really couldn't find anything similar on our side of town. Eventually, I married and had my own children and they too became Canter's fans.

As my dad aged, Canter's was often the highlight of his week. My children and I would pick him up on the weekend and make the drive. Sometimes, if his craving couldn't wait, he'd have his caretaker drive him there during the week. He always enjoyed going and it was what he wanted served at his eightieth birthday celebration.

My father passed in 2016 and although he is no longer with us, I still make the trek. My kids drive and go on their own now. Someday I hope to introduce Canter's to my future grandchildren."

Margo

"Across the street from Canter's Restaurant used to be Henry's Barber Shop at 430 N. Fairfax Avenue, which was in business at the same location for over forty years. Henry Goldscher passed away in 1997. He was an institution on Fairfax Avenue and cut hair until the day he died.

Henry's Barber Shop remained open by his sons Herschel and Allan, and his wife Tabby for five more years until it finally closed its doors. Henry took great pride in what he did and was inspired by the Canter family for their professionalism and determination to run a business with such love and devotion.

Henry proudly gave two of the Canter brothers their first haircuts when they were children and felt very humbled for doing so."

The Goldscher Family

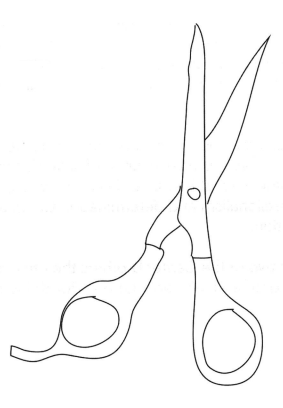

"My name is Richard John Jebejian. I was born July 18, 1942, on the 500 block of Martel Ave, two houses south of Melrose. Today I am seventy-six years young. In 1934 my father purchased our house for around $2,800. Just prior to World War II, the Melrose and Fairfax district was solely comprised of small family-owned businesses made up of a largely first-generation immigrant population that had recently arrived in the United States.

Melrose was like a United Nations. It was a mixture of all races, comprised of many small family-owned businesses, and Fairfax became a familiar place for many recently immigrated Jewish families before and after World War II. My family had a small upholstery shop where we recovered and made custom furniture for over eighty-five years. It was on the corner of Melrose and Martel throughout the 40s up through the late 80s.

For my entire life I have been a faithful customer of Canter's Deli. Canter's was a place my family regularly found itself for dinner to devour some phenomenal deli faire. My mother and her sisters would push my cousins and I up and down Melrose and Fairfax in strollers in the Forties and Fifties. We regularly wheeled into Canter's past the fresh baked goods with the whole family in tow.

As I grew into my adolescent years, Canter's became the place for us neighborhood locals to scarf down late-night meals or take dates after the Gilmore Drive-In Movies on Saturday nights. If you haven't heard of the Gilmore Drive-in before, that's because it is now the Grove parking lot. Our little neighborhood has changed quite a bit over the years.

changed in my seventy-six years. It's as if time has stood still when you enter either one of them. In the morning, Canter's caters to a small group of senior men that come in and have coffee, a Danish, and read the paper. After midnight, it serves punk rockers until the sun rises. I hope this never changes. These days I enjoy taking my wife, daughter, son, and now my grandson to Canter's. I have so many fond memories when I hear the words Canter's Deli. I think of Canter's Deli as one of the last truly family-owned restaurants left in Los Angeles.

Many years ago, I would go to Canter's with my new wife. There was a waitress named Big Mama. She was not a petite woman in stature, and she could dish out the sass just as well as she dished out the sandwiches and baked goods. It seems like just yesterday when she would walk over to our table and lovingly chastise my wife (who she called princess) about how she been waiting all week to find out how my wife wanted to change the menu today. This went on for years and we would not have had it any other way. She once said to me, "you know you could leave a tip," to which I replied, "Mama I always leave you a tip." With a wink and a smile, she told me that those tips might get her to Europe if she saved them up for thirty years, and was off to harassing someone else at another table. It was these off the cuff conversations, filled with humor, wit, and love, that have made me cherish my time spent in one of the booths at Canter's.

Over the years I have had the opportunity to meet the Canter family, Mr. and Mrs. Canter, Gary, and Jackie. I will always remember Gary, who has recently passed away. He would greet me with a big smile, a powerful handshake, and always welcomed me with a, 'How are you doing Buddy Buddy.' His younger sister Jackie and I have had the pleasure of working together for years. In addition to our family businesses, both of us love this neighborhood and have poured our souls into constantly improving the Melrose and Fairfax area for decades. I still go to Canter's every Friday around 7:00am for breakfast. I have my favorite waitress Anna, a surrogate mother if I have ever had one. She makes sure I always eat properly (no junk food in the morning), and that my coffee cup is never empty. She makes me feel like I am at home, having breakfast with my family.

I hope Canter's will continue to thrive and be around for eighty-seven more years at a minimum. One day I hope my grandson can have the same memorable experiences and great food that I have enjoyed for my whole life. Canter's is nothing short of an institution in this neighborhood. It has given Fairfax Avenue cache and class for many years. I wish Canter's, it's employees, and the Canter's family nothing but the best in years to come."

Richard, age 76

Alex Canter discovered his passion for restaurants at a very early age, spending most of his time implementing new technologies in the family deli. During his 4 years at the University of Madison, Wisconsin, Alex founded and led numerous startups. After returning to Los Angeles, he served as COO of an innovative platform for food truck booking. In 2017, he co-founded Ordermark to help restaurants maximize the benefits of online ordering by sending orders from multiple online ordering providers to a single device in the kitchen. Under his leadership, Ordermark helps thousands of restaurant brands nationwide to grow revenue with online ordering. He leads a growing team in Los Angeles and Denver, and received recognition for his achievement in building enterprise technology in the 2019 Forbes 30 under 30 list. He is a renown thought leader in the industry, and often speaks at conferences nationwide.

Gina Canter is an LA based artist who studied art and design at the University of Michigan. Gina has worked at local contemporary art galleries including Mouche Gallery in Beverly Hills. Throughout her studies, she experimented with modernity. In 2016, she won the Ross School of Business art competition with her 3 series Monet inspired rendition of the new business wing, Blau. She was recognized for her work by Steven Ross and Jeff Blau at the ribbon cutting and opening ceremony. The painting is framed in the wing. Graduating in 2017, she has since been creating a collection of acrylic portraits. In 2018, Gina was commissioned to create a 10-piece collection for a large enterprise client. This collection was featured at the Soho House Miami at Art Basel 2018. Her work continues to be featured nationwide—she most recently was commissioned for an NBA All-Stars 2019 event in Charlotte.

Photograph by Keiko Noah